FRESH THOUGHTS ON FOOD

The Author
Lynda Brown was joint-winner of the
Guardian/Mouton-Cadet Dinner Party
Competition in 1982, when the judges
particularly admired the freshness of her
cooking. An anthropologist by training,
Lynda Brown writes on cookery and
gardening. Her articles have appeared in
the *Guardian*, *Harpers & Queen* and the
Yorkshire Post. She lives in North
Yorkshire.

*This book will probably have to be reviewed
in the ordinary way, but between you and me
and the saucepan the proof of its excellence
lies in the eating.*

MAJOR HUGH B. C. POLLARD
The Sportsman's Cookery Book, 1926

Fresh Thoughts on Food

LYNDA BROWN

Dorling Kindersley

A Jill Norman Book

First published in hardback in 1986
by Chatto & Windus Ltd, 40 William IV Street, London WC2N 4DF

First published in paperback in 1988
by Dorling Kindersley Limited,
9 Henrietta Street, London WC2E 8PS

British Library Cataloguing in Publication Data
Brown, Lynda
  Fresh thoughts on food.
  1. Cookery, (Natural foods)
  I. Title
  641.5′637   TX741
  ISBN 0–86318–268–2

Printed in Great Britain by
Redwood Burn Ltd,
Trowbridge, Wiltshire

CONTENTS

PUBLISHER'S NOTE

Imperial and metric measurements are given in these recipes. When dealing with small quantities, 30 g is given as the approximate equivalent for 1 oz. For larger amounts this is no longer sufficiently accurate and adjustments have been made.

It should be remembered that the American pint is 16 fl oz in comparison to the Imperial pint, used in both Britain and Australia, which is 20 fl oz. The British standard tablespoon which has been used in this book holds 17.7 ml, the American 14.2 ml, and the Australian 20 ml. A teaspoon holds approximately 5 ml in all three countries.

ACKNOWLEDGEMENTS

This book has been a solitary affair, but it would not have been possible without the support and encouragement of the one who is near and dear to me. To my husband, Rick, I owe a special debt. I should like also to thank the staff at Darlington Library who, for five years, willingly and patiently provided me with so many books not found on our shelves today, and without whose help it would not have been possible to read and enjoy otherwise. To Gordon George, heart felt gratitude for a much needed burst of creativity at precisely the right moment.

I wish to acknowledge extracts quoted from the following books: X. M. Boulestin, *The Best of Boulestin*, Greenberg, New York, 1951; Rupert Croft-Cooke, *English Cooking*, W. H. Allen & Co., London, 1960; Elizabeth David, *French Provincial Cooking*, Michael Joseph, 1960; Alan Davidson, *North Atlantic Seafood*, Macmillan, London, 1979; Hannah Glasse, *The Art of Cookery Made Plain and Easy* (1796), S. R. Publications Ltd, 1971; Dorothy Hartley, *Food in England*, Macdonald & Co., London, 1954; Ambrose Heath, *A Menu For All Seasons*, Leslie Frewin Publishers Ltd, London, 1972; Ambrose Heath, *Vegetable Dishes and Salads*, Faber and Faber, London, 1938; M. Vivian Hughes, *A London Family 1870–1900*, Oxford University Press, 1946; William Wallace Irwin, *Gambols in Gastronomy*, Angus & Robertson, London, 1960; Florence B. Jack, *Cookery for Every Household*, T. C. & E. C. Jack, London, 1914; Tom Jaine, *Fish Times Thirty*, Dartmouth, 1980; Jessica Kuper (ed.), *The Anthropologist's Cookbook*, Routledge & Kegan Paul, London, 1977; *Edward Lear's Nonsense Omnibus*, F. Warne & Co. Ltd, London and New York, 1943; Mrs Hilda Leyel, *Green Salads and Fruit Salads*, George Routledge & Sons, London, 1935; A. A. Milne, *Not That It Matters*, Methuen & Co. Ltd, London, 1919; Major Hugh B. C. Pollard, *The Sportsman's Cookery Book*, Country Life Ltd, London, 1926; Edouard de Pomiane, *Cooking With Pomiane*, Bruno Cassirer, Oxford, 1962; Eleanour Sinclair Rohde, *Culinary and Salad Herbs*, Country Life Ltd, London, 1940; P. Morton Shand, *A Book of Food*, Jonathan Cape, London, 1927; Erroll Sherson, *The Book of Vegetable Cookery*, Frederick Warne & Co., London, 1931; Constance Spry, *Come Into The Garden, Cook*, J. M. Dent & Sons, London, 1942; *Success Cookery Book*, Success Publishing Company Ltd, London, 1932; Colin

Tudge *The Food Connection*, BBC Publications, London, 1985; Caroline Walker and Geoffrey Cannon, *The Food Scandal*, Century Publishing, London, 1984; Olof Wijk, *Eat At Pleasure, Drink By Measure*, Constable & Co. Ltd, London, 1970; Florence White, *Flowers as Food*, Jonathan Cape, London, 1934; Florence White, *Good Things In England*, Jonathan Cape, London, 1932.

And last, but by no means least, I should like to thank my editor, Hilary Laurie, who had the unenviable task of giving shape and form to an enormously large and wholly unruly manuscript.

Introduction

There is perhaps no science which has done more for the health and happiness of mankind than that of good cooking.

The provision of good and suitable food is a necessity to every form of life: it is required both to nourish the body and to keep it in good condition. Indeed, it is becoming more and more a recognised fact that health depends largely upon diet, and that cookery in its perfection is one of the most important factors in comfortable living.

FLORENCE B. JACK *Cookery for Every Household*, 1914

When, some years ago, I began cooking in earnest, I found to my dismay a culinary world divided into foods which were 'healthy' and therefore good for me, and those which were not. Cookery books were similarly divided. I could choose those offering nut rissoles and the like, or those whose recipes sounded full of promise but which paid scant regard to any nutritional principles. Convinced that good food could be both, I set out to adapt accepted methods of cooking accordingly.

I have a strong preference for fresh food, cooked without excessive fuss or elaboration. This is not new. It is a preference shared by other amateur and professional cooks who have been inspired and guided by writers like Elizabeth David. I am but one of many who cook with a book by Mrs David propped up on one side of the cooker and one by

Mrs Grigson on the other. But I also believe that good food should be good for you, a notion that has not been given the attention it deserves in most cookery books.

Throughout this book I try to break down the distinction between 'good' and 'healthy' food. It's a book for those who share my enthusiasm and who love to cook, but who also care that their food should be healthy. It is not a health food book in the accepted sense of the term. My stance is rather that most of what we eat is healthy but the way we cook that food is of paramount importance. You will find no insistence on brown rice over white, nor corn oil over butter. Neither will you meet the belief that fine food and good cooking need the prodigious quantities of butter, cream or salt that we have grown accustomed to. I maintain that food tastes better with far less of them.

For those of us who enjoy cooking, the real challenge is just beginning. That challenge is to translate current medical concern into practice and to produce the kind of food we genuinely enjoy, rather than food whose main virtue lies in its being good for us. I hope this book will show that, far from constraining our talents, responding to this challenge liberates them.

Fats, particularly dairy fats, sugar and salt have always had a high profile in cooking. In this book they do not – all are used sparingly. As a result, my food has a freshness and flavour no other style of cooking I have tried can match. Cooking and eating this way, my ability to taste and savour food has increased perceptibly, a skill which, as a cook, I cherish. It has enabled me to discover new tastes and combinations and it has added a new dimension to my cooking and enjoyment of food.

Of course there are disadvantages. Eating-out is now often a disappointment. Food is over-seasoned, sauces too rich, sweets unbearably sickly. In the kitchen stock cubes and other convenience foods no longer have a use. Their synthetic nature is disagreeable and I prefer to do without. Free-range eggs, fresh herbs and garden things become the order of the day. Like me, you too may end up growing your own.

Cooking with less fat, sugar and salt is easier than you might imagine and requires no radical change, only a little intelligent adaptation. It does not mean cooking with *no* fat, sugar and salt, nor does it mean a constant search for new recipes or acceptable substitutes. Almost invariably, a good recipe is better for less of these things. I use the same cookery books I have always used. I have a particular affection for English cookery writers, especially those writing in the first half of this century, and I find in them much of the inspiration I seek. This is as it should be. Treasured cook books, favourite authors and familiar dishes have a special place. We need simply to approach them in a slightly different, healthier way.

Do give yourself time to adapt. I discovered long ago that taste is primarily a function of habit. Salt is a perfect example of this. We pour it over our food indiscriminately, rarely bothering to taste first. We encourage our children by example. As cooks, we are taught that food without salt is bland and tasteless. We are never given a chance to discover what unsalted food is like. Our taste receptors become blunted and we cannot expect them to respond overnight to a change in the habits of a lifetime. You need an open mind and between two to six weeks to adapt to the change.

We are living, gastronomically speaking, at a time of great excitement and innovation. During the 1970s *nouvelle cuisine* provided a much needed catalyst and, whether or not we agree with some of the rather fanciful excesses that have followed in its wake, it has proved to be an advance from which we have all benefited. It would be churlish to deny that things have improved since I first forlornly contemplated and rejected bean stews and nut cutlets. There has been a tremendous shift in attitudes towards food. For the first time in culinary history we are, all of us, taking our diet much more seriously. Tastes are changing and the way we cook our food must change accordingly. Ask people what they want out of life and most will probably say health and happiness. As cooks, we can make a real contribution to both.

Cooking Tips

Faites simple   Escoffier

What a Frenchman intends these words to mean
may not be quite the same as what an English cook
would understand by them. They mean, I think, the
avoidance of all unnecessary complication and
elaboration: they do not mean skimping the work
or the basic ingredients, throwing together a dish
anyhow and hoping for the best. That is the crude
rather than the simple approach. To prove the
point, try simplifying a recipe which calls for rather
a lot of ingredients down to the barest essentials.
You may well find that the dish is more pleasing in
its primitive form, and then you will know that
your recipe was too fanciful. If, on the other hand,
the dish seems to lack savour, to be a little bleak or
insipid, start building it up again. By the end of this
process, you will have discovered what is essential
to that dish, what are the extras which enhance it,
and at what point it is spoilt by over-elaboration.
This system is also useful in teaching one how to
judge a recipe for oneself, instead of following it
blindly from a cookery book.

ELIZABETH DAVID *French Provincial Cooking*, 1964

COOKING WITH LESS FAT

Unless the recipe specifically demands it, I use the minimum amount of fat. In practice this means just enough butter or oil to coat the base of a medium sized pan, and for most purposes this works out at about ¼ oz / 7–8 g butter or a scant tablespoon of oil. When I refer to a knob of butter or a little oil, it is this quantity of fat I intend. Similarly, a good knob of butter is somewhere between ⅓–½ oz / 10–15 g. A little or a dribble of cream is anything between a teaspoon and a dessertspoon per person. Obviously you will have to use your own judgement: in a small pan, for small quantities, even less may be required; in a large pan, and for larger quantities, a little more.

Generally speaking, cooking with minimum quantities of fat poses no problems, but it does require a little initial adjustment and a little more care. Choose a heavy pan of the smallest size which will accommodate the food comfortably. If you use a pan larger than the amount of food requires, the risk of the food catching is greater. At all times regulate the heat carefully, and keep it gentle. When sweating vegetables, keep the heat low, cover the pan and stir the vegetables often, letting them cook in their own juices gently and evenly. When I fry meat, I find it better to use a little more fat and, once the meat has been sealed, to drain off what remains before proceeding.* As with any new skill, it is a question of practice and application.

THICKENING AGENTS

We have come to thank *nouvelle cuisine* for a whole new range of sauces, lighter, fresher and more elegant than their traditional counterparts, but still with substance and flavour. In the main, these sauces depend on the reduction of cooking juices or a thickening of egg yolks to provide body, with maybe a little cream or butter to give the desired softness. You will find examples of such sauces in this book.

When a simple thickener is called for, I find potato flour (*fécule*) to be the most satisfactory. It is no more than pure potato starch, virtually tasteless and requires no cooking out. Slake it first with a little cold water or milk and stir well before adding to the sauce. Add it, a teaspoon at a time, to hot but not boiling liquid, stirring thoroughly or whisking as you do so, until the desired thickness is achieved. The sauce will thicken immediately and is ready for use. It can be safely brought up to boiling point or simmered, but this is not necessary. Do not boil the

---

* Alternatively, by using a good quality non-stick pan, it is possible to seal meat without any additional fat.

thickened liquid vigorously. The potato flour changes texture and becomes unbearably gluey. This in no way affects the taste and can be remedied, to a certain extent, by diluting with a little extra liquid, but it spoils the texture. A generous teaspoon of potato flour will bind up to 10 fl oz / 300 ml of liquid, though I tend to use less. It adds virtually no calories to the dish.

SALT AND PEPPER

The majority of my recipes contain neither salt nor pepper. This is not to say that neither has a place in my kitchen, nor to deny their usefulness as seasonings. I regard them as two of the many seasonings we have at our disposal, to be used as and when necessary rather than from habit.

I have found that, for most cooking purposes, salt is entirely unnecessary, and that food is sweeter and fresher without it. In general, I find it necessary for pasta, pulses and most cereals, for oil-based sauces such as mayonnaise, and for poaching fresh fish. Now and then it may improve a sauce or a soup and, should this be the case, I have no hesitation in using it. As for the rest of my cooking, I now find it adds nothing but an unwelcome saltiness and so I prefer not to use it.

However, for those of you accustomed to salt, there is no merit in using it one day and banishing it the next. This can only lead to disenchantment. As likely as not, your food will taste very bland and your fears and prejudices will be confirmed. It is much more sensible to cut down gradually. Start by not adding salt until the final tasting of the dish. Do not salt the cooking water, and do not add any salt to dishes which contain ham, bacon, soy sauce or other salty foods. Many foods – meat, dairy products and some vegetables – are high in salt and require no more. Be critical but be fair. If you approach using less salt with an open mind, you will be surprised at how many dishes are not enhanced by it, and how quickly foods like bacon and salted butter seem unbearably salty. As you use these recipes, you will discover which foods you think need salt and which are better without. You will probably find that your list is longer than mine. In six months' time it may well be shorter.

I often read that, in order to make up for using less salt, we should use more herbs and other seasonings. I disagree. You have a better and fresher product. Why spoil it with bits and pieces that don't belong? Likewise, I see little point in salt substitutes. They taste dreadful.

BALANCE

Anyone who enjoys cooking instinctively makes the best use of colour, contrast and texture in food, but the overall nutritional balance of a meal is too often overlooked. When I'm planning a meal, I aim to include one protein element, one carbohydrate element, a small amount of fat, be it dairy or otherwise, and I fill in the rest with salads, fruit and vegetables. If the meal includes a refined carbohydrate such as white rice, I make sure that either the first or the last course and any accompanying vegetables are high in fibre. If I include butter or cream in any quantity in one course, I exclude them from others. If the protein element is a substantial helping of meat or fish, I am unlikely to include cheese at the same meal, whereas if the protein element is a vegetable, I usually add an egg for good measure. If the main course is heavy in calories, the other two will be light – a salad or vegetable to start with, and fruit of some kind to finish.

Most of us prefer the traditional pattern of three courses much of the time. But we need not approach them in the traditional way. In summer, for example, when our garden is in full production, dinner is often no more than a big bowl of salad followed by vegetables, with fruit or cheese to follow. Nor is it necessary to make protein the main dish or centrepiece of the meal. It can just as well start or finish with a protein dish – a pâté or potted fish or soufflé, a sweet omelette, and so on.

WEIGHTS AND MEASURES

Throughout, measurements are given in both metric and British Imperial. They are not interchangeable; use one or the other, but not both, in the same recipe. The conversions are never exact. One ounce is actually 28.350 grams, fine for a statistician but not much use to a cook. As is the accepted convention, I have taken one ounce as equivalent to 30 grams. With smaller quantities this is easily accurate enough but, with larger quantities this is no longer the case and further adjustments are necessary. As long as you work in either one of the systems, this is of no consequence because all the ingredients are in proportion.

QUANTITIES

Mrs Beeton held that, in order to reproduce 'esteemed dishes with certainty', all terms of indecision such as 'a bit of this, some of that, a small piece of that and a handful of the other' should be banned forthwith, and that all quantities 'be precisely and explicitly stated'. Marcel Boulestin thought exactly the reverse. 'What is the use of saying, when giving recipes for marmalade of apples "put in a quarter of a pound of sugar"? The apples may be either sweet or sour. It is better to say "put in a little sugar and add to taste till it is all right".' I can see merit in both sides of the argument and, like others faced with the dilemma of trying to take into account unseen ovens, the size of other people's appetites and just how big a medium onion should be, I have tried to strike a balance, concentrating on the feel of the dish and the effect one is aiming for. Final adjustments to taste and individual refinements are your prerogative.

Unless otherwise stated, recipes should serve four, bearing in mind that much will depend on the other elements in the meal and on the appetites of those you are feeding. Spoon measurements are level except when stated otherwise; a 'splash' is the same in any language.

A few Essentials

Then there are all your sauces, mustards, pickles,
chutneys, capers, salad-dressings and oils. Splendid.
So those cupboards are for tinned food and you
have selected them so that at any time you could
feed four people for a week on nothing else? You're
a wonder, Mrs Scoop; I wish there were more like
you.

RUPERT CROFT-COOKE *English Cooking,* 1960

HOME-MADE VINEGARS

These are so easy to make at home it hardly seems worth the bother of
buying them. It is clear from old cookery books they were once as much
a part of domestic life as was the making of bread. Raspberry and
elderberry vinegars kept out the cold and herb vinegars were used as
scents and revivers as well as in the kitchen.

One would not want every kind of flavoured vinegar, nor would one
wish to use them all the time, but two or three make a pleasant change
and a welcome addition to salads, sauces and the occasional soup.
Make them first in small quantities. Those which particularly appeal
can be made in larger amounts for use as and when required.

The method is always the same and takes only a minute. Stuff a bottle
or jar full of fresh herbs of your choice, fill up with a good quality white
wine vinegar and leave for a fortnight in a cool place. Strain through
muslin – not essential for herb vinegars, but better and a must for other
sorts of fruit or flower vinegars. Add a fresh sprig of herb if you like,
bottle, label and use as required.

Herb vinegars are best kept to a single herb, tarragon and basil being the most useful. Raspberry, blackberry, blackcurrant, elderflower (an exquisite vinegar) and lavender vinegar are all to be commended and are made in the same way.

HOME-MADE FRUIT LIQUEURS

These have many uses in fresh fruit salads, sweet omelettes, ice-creams or sorbets, or to flavour fruit purées and soufflés. Save the fruit to perk up winter salads, or as decorations for sweet and savoury dishes, or to eat on their own with a little of their liquor.

I follow Jane Grigson's instructions, given in her *Fruit Book*. For soft fruits, which are the simplest, fill a wide-mouthed jar full of perfect, unblemished fruit. Stone fruits such as cherries should be pricked first. Tip in caster sugar to come about a third of the way up the fruit and top up with the spirit of your choice – brandy, vodka, gin or Bacardi. Screw on the top and turn the jar back and forth to dissolve the sugar. Keep in a dark place and leave for at least a month before using. Check after a day or two to see that the sugar has completely dissolved. If not, an occasional shake should do the trick. Larger fruits should be sliced first and some of the kernels included, if you can be bothered. For firmer fruits, peaches, apricots or pears, for example, Mrs Grigson recommends making a thick syrup using twice the quantity of sugar to water and boiling for 5 minutes. Cool, pour in enough to come a third of the way up the fruit and top up with alcohol as before.

HOME-MADE YOGHURT

Home-made yoghurt has been part of my daily life for longer than I care to remember. It is simply made and so much better and cheaper than the commercial products available. It's an excellent substitute, at least in part, for cream.

To make your own yoghurt you need a bowl, a tablespoon of plain yoghurt to act as a starter, and somewhere with a constant temperature of around 45–50°C / 110–120°F to incubate the milk and turn it into yoghurt. Yoghurt makers and vacuum flasks fit the bill admirably but neither is strictly necessary. Instructions to wrap the bowl in blankets and leave it in the airing cupboard have always seemed to me to be both precarious and not a little fanciful. I make yoghurt, somewhat unconventionally, in the oven, an electric oven which holds its heat. Gas ovens and circotherm ovens do not work as well.

Bring 1 pint / 600 ml of milk to the boil, tip into a clean bowl and leave to cool down to a temperature of about 45°C / 110°F. To hurry things up, stand it in a bowl of cold water. Mix a tablespoon of plain yoghurt, well stirred to ensure an even distribution of bacteria, with a little of the cooled milk to form a thin cream. Stir this into the bowl of milk, making sure that all is thoroughly mixed. Meanwhile put the oven on very low until it feels just comfortably warm, 3 or 4 minutes. Turn off the oven, cover the bowl with cling film and transfer to the warmed oven to set. The yoghurt will take 5–6 hours, possibly a little less, to incubate. Check the oven after 3–4 hours. If it feels cold, reheat for a minute or two on the lowest setting. You will soon learn to judge how long to leave the yoghurt to develop the thickness and flavour you like. Cool and keep, covered, in the refrigerator.

Yoghurt culture thrives and grows fastest within the temperature range 30–50°C / 80–120°F. It can take anything from 3 to 8 hours, depending on the initial temperature of the milk and of the incubator. Disturb it as little as possible during incubation. The longer yoghurt is left to incubate, the sharper and more acid the taste will become and the more the whey will separate out. You must, therefore, experiment to establish the time and temperature that produce yoghurt to your taste. For continuing good results, make your next batch whilst the present yoghurt is fresh, within three days, and make sure you stir it well.

Home-made yoghurt tends to be thinner than commercial yoghurt which is made with a high proportion of skimmed milk. This has implications when it comes to using yoghurt for cooking (see below). Should you prefer a thicker yoghurt, either stir in up to 2 oz / 60 g skimmed milk powder per 1 pint / 600 ml of milk, or simmer the milk until it has reduced in volume by at least a quarter and preferably a half.

Nutritionally, yoghurt has all the benefits of milk and more. It is a very easily digested form of milk, taking something like 30–40 minutes instead of the usual 3–4 hours. The calorific content of yoghurt ranges from 75 cals / 5 fl oz / 150 ml for plain 'low fat' yoghurt to about 100 cals / 5 fl oz / 150 ml for whole milk yoghurt. Fortified milk yoghurt will obviously contain more.

COOKING WITH YOGHURT

People have cooked with yoghurt for centuries. It adds a pleasing acidity to dishes, is useful as a marinade and as a substitute for cream. Unless it is to be cooked for any length of time or is boiled vigorously, it will not curdle and does not need stabilising first. Beat it smooth and add gradually to the sauce at the end or towards the end of cooking.

A thick yoghurt is generally preferable to a thin one, particularly for sauces and dips. This is simply achieved. Tip the yoghurt into a sieve lined with muslin and drain off the whey until the desired thickness is reached. Alternatively, gently squeeze the whey out of the muslin using your hands. The yoghurt will be the consistency of double cream or thicker and will hold its shape. It can be incorporated into sauces and dressings without making them watery.

In this book, where thick yoghurt is called for, I mean yoghurt which has been drained of its excess whey. For hot sauces, commercial yoghurt is usually thick enough and this is the thickness you should aim for with your home-made yoghurt. For cold sauces where the yoghurt gives both lightness and body, aim to drain it until it is very thick – the type of sauce will obviously guide you. Should you have drained the yoghurt a little too much, a little of the drained whey can always be re-incorporated. Used this way, yoghurt is an excellent adjunct to and base for any number of sauces. All the recipes in this book have been tested with home-made yoghurt.

HOME-MADE TOMATO SAUCES

A home-made tomato sauce is one of the nicest and most useful of sauces. It's worth making in quantity when fresh tomatoes are at their cheapest, to put down in the freezer, ready to use with fish, meat, vegetables and pasta, or as a base for soups and other made-up dishes. How you make it is entirely up to you, the term is purely descriptive. Tomato sauce is a family of sauces ranging from, at its simplest and freshest, chopped ripe tomatoes briefly tossed in butter or oil until the juices run, to the dark robust Italian sauces for spreading on pizzas and serving on pasta.

Where a light, fresh-tasting sauce is required, fresh tomatoes are a must. For other types, canned tomatoes make an excellent sauce. A scrap of sugar or tomato purée is usually a good idea. A few drops of basil vinegar can give a wonderful lift. Skinning tomatoes beforehand is a matter of personal taste. For sauces which are to be sieved it is unnecessary, but probably wise for unsieved ones. A great fuss is made about the value of the skins and the contribution they make to the flavour of the sauce. In my experience, it is the quality of the tomatoes and not their skins which makes the difference.

As an approximate guide, 1 lb / 450 g tomatoes should yield about 10 fl oz / 300 ml of sieved sauce.

FOUR TOMATO SAUCES

The basics: olive oil or butter for frying, as appropriate; chopped, very ripe tomatoes, skinned or not as required (see note above), or canned tomatoes.

Optional ingredients: small onion finely chopped; crushed clove(s) of garlic; small piece of celery, finely chopped; small carrot, finely chopped; diced bacon.

Optional flavourings: savoury butters – tarragon, basil, chervil or dill; pinch of sugar; tomato purée; fresh parsley, basil, mint, oregano, dill, fennel; dried oregano or marjoram; bay leaves; coriander seeds; dried chillies; basil vinegar; port, marsala, red or white wine; black pepper.

Sauce one
Elizabeth David's 3 minute tomato sauce: melt a knob of butter in a small heavy pan, or alternatively a teaspoon each of butter and olive oil. Add skinned and roughly chopped tomatoes and cook gently for about 3 minutes until they are hot and the juices have begun to run. Season with a pinch of sugar and a sprinkling of finely chopped herbs. Serve as an accompaniment to meat and fish dishes, as a sauce over savoury crêpes, or as a filling for tomato omelettes.

An alternative and equally pleasing sauce can be made by melting a couple of pats of savoury butter and cooking the tomatoes as above, gently shaking the pan to distribute the flavours. Use immediately.

Sauce two
1 lb / 450 g ripe, sweet tomatoes; small onion finely chopped; clove of garlic (optional); pinch of sugar; few drops of basil vinegar (optional). Melt a knob of butter or a little olive oil in a pan and gently sweat the onion until soft and limpid. Add the garlic if used, together with the roughly chopped tomatoes and a pinch of sugar. Continue cooking, fairly briskly, for 5–10 minutes until the tomatoes have formed a discernible sauce. Sieve, check the seasoning and use as required.

This produces a thinnish purée of good, fresh flavour and colour, and is an excellent base for tomato soups and other dishes where tomato sauce is an ingredient. One or two basil leaves, added with the tomatoes and removed before sieving, are a worthwhile addition. Unsieved, it makes a good chunky purée to mix with cooked vegetables. By altering the flavourings, a whole range of sauces, each slightly different, can be produced from this basic formula.

Sauce three

Make a tomato sauce as above, adding two or three large sprigs of mint with the tomatoes. At the end of the cooking time, remove the mint, sieve, return to the pan and continue cooking until the sauce is as thick as required, adding a little tomato purée if necessary. The mint gives the sauce a lovely fresh tang. Excellent with charcoal grilled lamb, aubergines, courgettes and savoury meat and fish croquettes.

Sauce four

1 medium onion, finely sliced; 1–2 cloves of garlic, crushed; 1 lb / 450 g fresh tomatoes, or large can of tinned tomatoes; 1–2 dessertspoons tomato purée; small glass of red or white wine; ½ stick of celery; hefty pinch of dried oregano plus fresh oregano, basil, or parsley; bay leaf; olive oil for frying.

Sweat the onion and garlic till soft. Add the rest of the ingredients and cook steadily for 30–40 minutes until the sauce has reduced and has a good robust flavour. Remove the celery and bay leaf, sieve through a *mouli*, check the seasoning making the usual adjustments. Add extra fresh herbs if you wish, and use as required.

A sauce of character for pasta and pizzas. It can be reduced further or put through a blender, if preferred. Bacon can be added with the onions if that is to your taste.

FRESH HERBS

Most herbs are obligingly easy to grow, dividing neatly into two broad groups – the more delicate annuals for summer use and the robust, stronger tasting perennials which withstand the winter. Many need little in the way of care and attention. Anyone with even the smallest of gardens will profit from a few herbs tucked in, here and there, where space will allow. If necessary, they can be grown in pots on a kitchen window sill or balcony.

I find a few fresh herbs indispensable. In summer, basil, dill, tarragon, mint, coriander, savory and oregano; in winter, thyme, parsley, sage and the occasional sprig of rosemary; in early spring, the first bright green of sorrel, chives and chervil. Each brings its own distinctive charm.

You do not need a large quantity of herbs, or a complete range. Half a dozen of those you like will serve you better than two dozen of those you find you use but now and then. Nor should herbs dominate your cooking. Over-enthusiasm, a herbs-with-everything approach, can be as unattractive as cooking which has never known a hint of fresh greenery.

SPROUTED BEANS, GRAINS AND SEEDS

These can be a valuable addition to our diet, and are especially useful in all kinds of salads or lightly cooked as a vegetable.

Any grain/seed/bean can be sprouted. It's best to start with mung beans (Chinese bean sprouts) or whole lentils. These are the easiest. Pick over the beans and remove any broken ones, grit etc. and rinse thoroughly. Fill a wide-mouthed jar about a quarter full and cover the beans with fresh water to a depth of about 3 in / 7.5 cm. Leave overnight to soak and swell. Next morning tip the beans into a sieve and rinse under running water. Drain them, shaking off all the excess water, return to the jar, cover with cling film and leave in a warm place to sprout, about three days. Rinse them every morning as before and check occasionally that they do not dry out. They should be kept moist but not wet – wet seeds are liable to rot.

Sprouts grow fastest without light and in a temperature around 20°C / 70°F. A warm kitchen is fine. I keep mine in a brown paper bag in a cupboard, though they will also happily sprout on the window sill, and dark conditions are not essential. For maximum nutritional value use them when the sprouts are ½–1 in / 1–2.5 cm long. Check and discard any seeds which have not sprouted. Mung beans in particular are bullet hard and most unpleasant. Store any surplus in the refrigerator in an airtight container. They will keep for 4–5 days.

Sprouts are very economical. A handful of dried beans will yield a jar full of sprouts. They have a crunchy texture and sweetish flavour which reflects the parent bean. Chick peas are particularly good sprouted. Others to try are aduki beans, wheat grains and sunflower seeds. Tiny seeds like alfalfa and sesame seeds are fiddlier (use just a tablespoon), take a little more care but make a change. Experiment to find which you like and find useful.

Bread

'Do you mean to tell me,' he exclaimed, 'that this thing is only flour and water?' Holding it up in amazement, he added, 'Then what on earth do they do to the bread in the shops?'

M. VIVIAN HUGHES *A London Home in the Nineties*, 1946

Thanks to an energetic consumer campaign in the late 60s and 70s, we can at last buy decent bread. Yet nothing we buy can compare with home-baked bread or equal the pleasure it brings. The reason is simple. Modern large-scale bread baking, both brown and white, is a streamlined, highly mechanical process, geared to minimum time and maximum yield, collecting on its way an absurdly long list of preservatives, stabilisers, emulsifiers, dough improvers, yeast stimulants and who knows what else. By contrast, baking bread at home has hardly changed for centuries and requires nothing more than flour, yeast, water and time. Is it any wonder ours is a better, more satisfying product?

Making bread is a straightforward business. Unlike a soufflé or a sauce, bread demands little attention, no set time-scale, and no particular skills to get it right. Left alone, it will almost make itself, and as long as one or two basic rules are adhered to, the loaf you bake and the way you bake it can be as varied as you want. The one thing you must watch is the temperature of the liquid which should be never more than tepid, around 37–38°C / 98–100°F. Yeast cells begin to die off at higher temperatures. The first couple of times you make bread, measure this with a thermometer. Thereafter, a mixture of one third boiling water and two thirds cold, together with a quick finger check, is all that's required. For the rest, it's simply a question of finding the five minutes or so to start the dough off and put it in the tins when it's ready.

The flour you use is important. Much of the quality and flavour of your bread will depend on this. Freshly stone-ground flour, from organically grown English wheat, undeniably produces the sweetest, best bread, be it brown or white. Fortunately, such flour is now produced by independent millers up and down the country. Look out for it and buy it whenever you get the chance, storing it in a cool place out of the kitchen.

Bread is indeed our staff of life. The grain of wheat from which it comes is tough, durable and a warehouse full of goodness which has sustained mankind for some 6000 years. Apart from its fibre content, wholewheat bread supplies protein, useful amounts of B vitamins, one of the best sources of vitamin E, ten different minerals and around one hundred and fifty first-class calories in each average slice. Value for money at any price.

MY BASIC LOAF

This is a combination of both old and new – an initial sponging of the dough, followed by a straightforward proving and baking without any intermediate rises. It differs from other, standard recipes in two other respects. Firstly, it contains half the usual recommended amount of salt. I find this amount of salt makes no difference to the quality of the bread. Any more now produces a loaf too salty for my taste. Indeed, I am coming to the conclusion that salt is unnecessary in wholemeal bread.

Secondly, I now use Fermipan, an activated form of dried yeast. Unlike fresh or ordinary dried yeast, it requires no preliminary creaming or reconstituting. It's simply stirred into the flour or sprinkled on top of the liquid and gives excellent results every time. Because of its potency, little is required. At the time of writing 1 oz / 30 g cost approximately 12 p, enough for up to ten batches of bread. Like all dried yeast it keeps indefinitely and is one modern convenience I can recommend. Should you prefer to use fresh yeast, allow $\frac{1}{3}$–$\frac{1}{2}$ oz / 10–15 g. Cream it first with a little of the tepid water and a pinch of sugar, leave for 10–15 minutes to become frothy, adding it to the dough with the liquid. Dried yeast needs to be reconstituted in the same way.

As a general guideline 1 oz / 30 g fresh yeast = $\frac{1}{2}$ oz / 15 g ordinary dried yeast = $\frac{1}{3}$ oz / 10 g Fermipan or approx. 3 teaspoons. I use less yeast than most recipes call for; but it's simple to add a little extra if you prefer.

For 2 large loaves: 2 lb / 900 g wholewheat flour, or for a lighter loaf, 1 lb 12 oz / 780 g wholewheat flour plus 4 oz / 120 g strong, unbleached white flour or 2 lb / 900 g 85% wheatmeal flour; teaspoon salt; 2 tablespoons sunflower or safflower oil; 1–2 teaspoons of sweetener – honey, malt, molasses or brown sugar; approx. 1 pint / 600 ml tepid water; 1 generous teaspoon Fermipan; 2 large, greased bread tins.

Set 2–3 oz / 60–90 g of flour aside. Mix the rest with the salt in a large bowl and warm through in a very low oven for a few minutes. Make a well in the centre, add the sugar, oil and water and sprinkle the Fermipan on top. Incorporate other sorts of yeast in the usual way. Beat in enough flour to make a thick batter, something like a mud pie, and sprinkle some of the remaining flour over the top to form a crust. Now leave the batter to sponge in a warm place for at least 30 minutes or until it has expanded and become sponge-like and breaks through the crust. It is this initial sponging which I find particularly valuable for wholewheat bread. It renders the dough soft and pliable and cuts the work of kneading in half whilst allowing the yeast time to work.

Incorporate the rest of the flour, using the extra set aside if needed, and briefly knead the dough for 4–5 minutes until smooth. It should not feel wet or sticky. Divide into half and put into 2 large, greased bread tins. Slash the top, cover with a damp cloth or put in a large plastic bag and leave in a warm place to prove and double in bulk. The dough should reach the top of the tins. Bake in a fairly hot oven 200°C / 400°F / gas mark 6 for about 40 minutes or until the bottom of the loaf sounds hollow when tapped. Return to the turned-off oven to crisp the sides and cool on a rack.

Alternatively, the bread can be started in a cool oven. This works particularly well with these under-proved doughs. Switch the oven on at 200°C / 400°F / gas mark 6, put the bread in and cook as before. I often use this method myself.

This basic bread can be varied in any number of ways. Increasing the proportion of white flour to 8 oz / 225 g gives a considerably lighter loaf which some may prefer for their everyday bread, and doubling the amount of sweetener to a tablespoon produces a markedly sweeter one. The oil, too, can be dispensed with or replaced by other fats. Substituting 2–3 oz / 60–90 g of rye, barley, oatmeal or buckwheat flour, or even cooked potato, for some of the usual flour, produces loaves of different characters worth trying.

A MASLIN LOAF

A bread of character, full-bodied, dense and dark, made from a mixture of rye and wheat meals and with a sour dough starter. Such bread was the standard British loaf for everyone except the rich or fortunate until well into the eighteenth century.

1 lb / 450 g wholemeal flour; 8 oz / 225 g rye flour; 8 oz / 225 g strong unbleached white flour; 1 teaspoon Fermipan; 1 teaspoon salt; 1 teaspoon molasses; sour dough starter (see method); approx. 18 fl oz / 500 ml tepid water.

Two or three days before you want to start the bread, mix 3 tablespoons of rye flour with enough milk to make a thick paste, cover with cling film and leave in a warm place to ripen. When ready it will smell pleasantly sour. This contributes to the bread's characteristic flavour, reminiscent of those excellent continental rye breads.

Mix the flours and salt in a large bowl and put to warm for a few minutes in a very low oven. Make a well in the centre, add the molasses, sour dough starter and water, and stir in the Fermipan. Sponge as for the previous recipe and leave for 2–3 hours, or longer if it suits. This is a bread which cannot be hurried; at all times the dough is left to ripen and mature slowly. Draw in the rest of the flour and knead until the dough feels malleable, adding a little more if the dough seems too sticky. Stickiness is a feature of all rye doughs, so don't worry over much and just use your judgement. Cover with a damp cloth and leave for a minimum of 12 hours and anything up to 24 hours. I tend to start the bread in the afternoon of one day and bake it sometime the following morning, leaving it overnight in the warmth of the sitting room. Check that the cloth does not dry out too much, otherwise the dough can form an unwelcome crust. Knock back the dough and divide the mixture between 2 large, greased loaf tins and prove as in the previous recipe. Bake for about 45–50 minutes in a fairly hot oven 200°C / 400°F / gas mark 6, or until the loaves sound hollow when tapped. Return to the turned-off oven for a few minutes to crisp the sides, and cool on a rack.

This makes a fine, richly flavoured loaf which keeps well and should be eaten in thin slices. It's especially good toasted. Keep back a lump of dough to use as your next sour dough starter. Cover with milk and protect with cling film as before. Left in the warmth of the kitchen it will keep quite happily for a week or so.

SEMOLINA TEA-TIME BREAD

A favourite bread of mine and no trouble to do. Wholewheat semolina makes an excellent loaf with a slightly gritty texture. This one is Italian in origin, a bread with a sweetish flavour and cake-like texture. Neither this nor the bread that follows, *bioja*, needs salt. I have made them both several times with and without salt and can find no real difference in flavour. Both breads seemed to be slightly sweeter when the salt was omitted.

For 1 loaf: 8 oz / 225 g wholewheat semolina; 6 oz / 170 g strong, unbleached white flour; 2 tablespoons olive oil; 1 egg, lightly beaten; 1 tablespoon honey; scant teaspoon Fermipan; approx. 5 fl oz / 150 ml tepid water; ½ teaspoon salt (optional).

Mix together the flours and the salt, if used, in a large bowl. Make a well in the centre, add the egg, honey, olive oil and warm water and sprinkle the yeast on top. Mix in the usual way to a softish dough adding a little more water or flour as appropriate, and knead briefly until smooth. This won't be as pliable as ordinary dough but should still have a certain amount of elasticity. Form into a ball and place on a greased baking sheet or, better, inside a 7 in / 18 cm sponge tin. Make a couple of slashes across the top, cover with a damp cloth and leave in a warm place until it has doubled in bulk (2–3 hours). Bake for 25–30 minutes in a moderate oven, 180°C / 350°F / gas mark 4 until nicely browned and the loaf sounds hollow when tapped. Cool on a rack and eat fresh.

CARIBBEAN COCONUT CORN BREAD (*Bioja*)

An unusual bread, from the *Sunday Times Book of Real Bread* by Elisabeth Lambert Ortiz. Not a breakfast loaf, but one to serve with a vegetarian meal instead of potatoes or other carbohydrate, or for tea-time. Although you'd never guess, it's also as high in fibre as wholewheat bread. I have reduced the fat content and made one or two other minor amendments.

6 oz / 170 g strong, unbleached white flour; 4 oz / 120 g cornmeal; 2 oz / 60 g finely grated, fresh coconut or 1 oz / 30 g desiccated coconut; 1 large, ripe banana, mashed; ½ teaspoon ground allspice; 1 tablespoon honey; 5 fl oz / 150 ml warm milk; 1 oz / 30 g melted butter; scant teaspoon of Fermipan; ½ teaspoon salt (optional); extra water.

Mix the flours and salt, if used, in a large bowl. Wholefood shops now stock an unrefined cornmeal which I generally use. Make a well in the centre, pour in the warm milk, sprinkle over the yeast and draw in enough flour to make a thick batter. Cover with some of the remaining flour and leave to sponge in the usual way for a couple of hours in a warm place. Beat in the rest of the ingredients to form a stiff batter, adding a little more tepid water if necessary. Transfer the mixture to a greased tin – the shape is not important but choose one which is large enough to allow the dough to expand – and leave in a warm place until well risen and doubled in bulk. Bake in a moderate oven 180°C / 350°F / gas mark 4 for about 40–45 minutes until the surface is well browned and the bread has shrunk slightly from the sides. Cool in the tin for a few minutes and then turn out on to a rack.

It is well worth using fresh coconut. Bore a small hole in the base and let out the watery liquid which can be drunk. Lightly grill the skin, turning the shell round so that all sides are exposed to the heat. This contracts the shell and makes the flesh easier to extract. Using a hammer break the coconut in half (it will probably smash into several pieces) and prise out the flesh. Rinse it if necessary to remove any charred bits from the shell, and either grate it by hand or blend in a food processor for a few seconds. The flesh is beautifully sweet. It freezes well and defrosts in a matter of seconds.

PITTA BREAD

Home-made pitta bread is so good and so easy that I wonder why anyone bothers to buy it. I usually make a batch when I'm making white bread, using half the dough for a loaf and half for pittas which I freeze and use as required.

Suppose you have a quantity of bread dough ready for baking. Knock the dough back and divide it into 3–4 oz / 90–120 g pieces. Using a liberal amount of flour, roll out each piece to form a characteristic pitta shape, longer than it is wide, and approximately $\frac{1}{4}$ in / $\frac{1}{2}$ cm thick. It's the thickness which is crucial: too thin and the pittas cook like a biscuit and do not puff out to form their characteristic pouch; too thick and they're no longer pittas. Place on greased and floured baking sheets, cover with a damp cloth, and leave to prove in a warm place for about 15 minutes. On top of the stove is ideal. The damp cloth is also important, for at all times you want to prevent a crust from forming which would impede the cooking. Bake in a very hot oven 230°C / 450°F / gas mark 8 for 7–8 minutes. As soon as they puff out and smell cooked, they are ready. Don't be tempted to cook them longer. Remove and serve immediately in the traditional style, slashed diagonally into thick slices. If you're making a batch to eat later, wrap them in a cloth to keep them soft, and reheat later in foil as required.

A basic bread dough made from 1 lb / 450 g flour, approximately ½ pint / 300 ml tepid water, ½ teaspoon salt, a scant teaspoon of Fermipan, and a tablespoon of olive oil (optional), and mixed in the usual way for white bread, will yield about six pittas.

BREAD TARTLETS WITH SAVOURY FILLINGS

We are accustomed to serving large pizzas as a main course, and very good they are too. But have you ever thought of making individual tarts from small quantities of dough, and filling them, not with the standard tomato and cheese mixtures, but with those more commonly found in pastry-based tarts and pies? The bread base makes them lighter and healthier, and they are easily assembled from a little of the dough set aside when making white or a light wheatmeal bread. Alternatively, make a batch of pizza dough from 8 oz / 225 g flour, 1–2 tablespoons olive oil, a little salt, a teaspoon of Fermipan, and enough tepid water (approx. 5 fl oz / 150 ml) to form a pliable dough. Freeze what you do not use for the next time. Such tarts make an admirable first course, a pleasant change from soups or other hot starters.

The procedure is simple. Pinch off not more than 2 oz / 60 g portions of dough after it has been left to rise and is ready to be knocked back. Shape as for rolls and place, either on an oiled baking sheet or—better—in a Yorkshire pudding tray. Using your hands, tease the dough out to form rounds exactly as you would a pizza. It is important to keep the base very thin. Fill the centre with the slightly warmed filling, brush the edges with olive oil and leave in a warm place to prove for about 15 minutes. Dribble a teaspoon of olive oil across the filling of each tart and bake in a very hot oven, 230°C / 450°F / gas mark 8, for 10–12 minutes. Serve immediately, allowing one per person.

Pissaladière filling
The classic French filling.

1¼ lb / 570 g onions, peeled and finely sliced; 2 tablespoons olive oil; 2 smallish tomatoes, skinned and chopped.

Cook the onions in the olive oil in a heavy covered pan until soft and golden, taking care that they do not catch or brown. Add the tomatoes and continue cooking, with the lid slightly ajar, until both have amalgamated into a thick purée, about 45–50 minutes. Allow to cool until tepid. Fill each tart generously with some of the mixture and decorate with thin slivers of anchovy fillet and half a stoned olive in the centre. Allow to prove, then bake. This quantity should fill about 8 tartlets. It's not worth making less, so freeze any surplus, or use for other dishes. Onion fondue (p. 71) can also be used.

Chard, pork, and parsley filling
Another excellent, simply made, French filling, based on the one given in Jane Grigson's *Vegetable Book*.

4 oz / 120 g Cumberland sausage; 10–12 oz / 280–340 g Swiss chard or spinach beet leaves; crushed and chopped clove of garlic (optional); chopped parsley.

Wash the chard or spinach beet and cook briefly over a high heat in a little water until wilted and just softened. Drain, squeeze out the excess moisture, and chop to a roughish purée. Skin the sausage and cook in an ungreased pan until it begins to brown, breaking the meat up with a fork or the back of a wooden spoon. Add the chopped leaves, and the garlic if used, and continue to cook for another 5 minutes, stirring everything about from time to time. Season with plenty of chopped parsley and allow to cool until tepid. Fill and bake as before. Sufficient for 4 tartlets.

Soups

A woman who cannot make soup should not be allowed to marry.

P. MORTON SHAND *A Book of Food*, 1927

Soups make a welcome start to any meal, offering scope and variety for even the most inexperienced cook. A simple potato and onion broth can form the basis of a mild and refreshing cucumber soup (p. 40), of a summery purée speckled with fresh herbs or, with the addition of cabbage, olive oil and some good coarse Italian sausage, a sustaining soup for winter. Hefty bean and pasta soups, gazpacho, soups made from garlic, fruit or almonds, fish soups, delicate vegetable purées garnished with a few crunchy croûtons, chowders, broths and sparkling clear consommés – the culinary world is full of good soups made from ingredients already in the larder along with a few fresh vegetables, or simply water and a few well-chosen flavourings. The majority of soups in this chapter are of this kind. I confess I have neither time or patience for grander affairs. Most take but five minutes' work and less than half an hour to cook. All have served me well whatever the occasion and whoever the company.

As I cook more, my fondness for soups grows rather than diminishes. They are above all companionable things. True, they may not tax our creative skills in the way that sauces do. Perhaps they are a little mundane, but there is still no finer beginning, nor anything which is so warmly received. Accompanied by some freshly baked bread and who could want more?

STOCKS

Basic stocks need no introduction and for most soups are neither necessary or desirable. In general, water is the perfect base and is what I use myself most of the time. However, two which I find very useful are these:

Chinese broth

The Chinese use assorted meat bones and no vegetable flavourings to make their stocks. This produces excellent results: a clean-tasting broth of good flavour which keeps well, and which forms an admirable base for light, delicate soups such as vegetable consommés, as well as for all Chinese dishes.

1 meaty chicken carcass, or a boiling fowl; 1–1½ lb / 450–675 g pork spare ribs; 12 oz / 340 g ham, bacon, or beef bones; water; onion skins (optional).

Proportions are 2 : 2 : 1 of chicken : pork : ham, bacon or beef bones, though I prefer less ham or bacon. Cover the bones with three times their depth of water. Bring slowly to the boil, skim, and simmer 3–4 hours, or until the broth is of a good flavour, skimming as necessary. The onion skins give a lovely amber tinge. Strain, remove the fat and the broth is ready to use. It will keep 3–4 days in the refrigerator.

The method adapts well for smaller quantities, a few chicken wings and a piece of bacon providing enough broth for an evening's soup. A small piece of fresh ginger adds to the Chinese flavour.

Prawn stock

Discarded prawn shells and legs, as available; clove of garlic, crushed; piece of leek, carrot, celery; sprig of basil or parsley; fresh tomato or a little tomato purée; 1 tablespoon olive oil.

Sweat the diced vegetables, garlic and prawn shells in the oil for about 5 minutes in a covered pan. Pour on enough water to cover, add the herbs and tomato or purée and simmer for 30–40 minutes. Strain, pressing hard against the sieve to extract all the juices and use as required.

The stock has a decidedly sweet quality and will taste more or less of shellfish depending on the size of your initial hoard of shellfish debris. It makes a fine base for any number of soups (see particularly *sopa d'ajo*, p. 36), for risottos and for fish sauces where a hint of the Mediterranean is called for. An excellent and useful stock.

INSTANT ORIENTAL SOUP

This is not so much a recipe as a way of producing any number of delicately flavoured broths in no time to speak of and at hardly any cost. Over the years I have made countless versions of this soup, each one slightly different. One of the most useful recipes to know about and build on.

Aim to use no more than 6 or 7 ingredients. You need some from group 1 to give body to the soup, and some from group 2 to give an added freshness and sweetness. It is important that these should be added at the last moment. Those from group 3 add a protein element, which changes the character slightly to give a more 'meaty' feel.

1 – a selection from: carrots, leeks, celery, turnips, all cut into thin *julienne* strips; frozen peas; thinly sliced mushrooms; Chinese noodles; bean sprouts.

2 – a selection from: shredded lettuce leaves; thinly sliced cucumber; chopped spring onions; shredded celery leaves; wedges of tomato; thinly sliced water chestnuts; sprigs of watercress; few drops of sesame oil.

3 – optional ingredients: lightly beaten egg; minced cooked pork or chicken; chopped prawns.

Bring about 1 pint / 600 ml of water to the boil and add 1–2 tablespoons of soy sauce. Cook the vegetables chosen from group 1 until just tender, about 3–5 minutes. Add those from group 2, and one from group 3, if used. Bring to the boil, check the seasoning (you may need a little extra soy sauce) and serve. The quantity of ingredients required for these broths is tiny. For 4 servings, allow about $1–1\frac{1}{2}$ oz / 30–45 g of carrots, leeks, celery or turnip; 2 oz / 60 g peas; a couple of mushrooms, tomatoes or water chestnuts; about 1 oz / 30 g of noodles; 2 or 3 shredded lettuce leaves; a quarter of a cucumber; 2 spring onions; a few sprigs of watercress; 1 egg; 2–3 oz / 60–90 g meat and half a dozen prawns. These are intended as a guide only. Precise quantities are not important. Use your judgement and what you have to hand.

You do not have to use water. A light chicken stock or some Chinese broth, with one or two flavouring ingredients – say spring onions, wedges of tomato, a few peas, or best of all, just a few slices of thinly cut cucumber – produces a simple but memorable soup.

SOPA D'AJO

A family favourite. Not a grand soup but an unctuous, garlicky broth and a great standby when both time and ingredients are on the short side. Try and use shellfish stock, for its distinctive sweetness marries well with the garlic. The consistency of the finished soup is a matter of personal taste and will depend on how much bread you use, so be prepared to adjust the liquid accordingly. Spanish recipes usually include a teaspoon of paprika, to be stirred in, off the heat, after the preliminary browning. I rarely bother with this myself.

1¼ pint / 750 ml shellfish or robust fish stock, flavoured with 1–2 tablespoons of tomato purée; 2 thin slices of wholewheat bread; 2 fat cloves of garlic, finely chopped; 1 tablespoon finely chopped parsley; olive oil for frying.

Choose a smallish saucepan and gently soften the garlic in a tablespoon or so of olive oil. Add the bread, roughly broken up, and continue frying for a few minutes, stirring frequently. The bread will break up and brown somewhat. Pour on the stock, simmer for 15–20 minutes and, just before serving, stir in a tablespoon of finely chopped parsley. A chopped tomato added with the stock makes a good addition.

LEMON AND CHERVIL SOUP

A variation on the *avgolemono* theme, very fresh and pretty to look at – primrose yellow, speckled with green, and carpeted in billowy foam. A good choice before roast game or grilled lamb, or whenever a delicate fish broth of quality happens to be at hand.

1 pint / 600 ml fish stock; 1 tablespoon rice; juice of 1 large lemon beaten together with two eggs; 1 tablespoon finely chopped chervil.

Simmer the rice in the fish stock in a covered pan until tender. Have the lemon and egg mixture ready in a bowl, add a ladleful of soup and whisk together. Return this mixture to the pan, keep whisking and cook until the mixture thickens slightly but on no account let it boil. Stir in the chervil and serve immediately.

ANDALUSIAN ALMOND SOUP

Not surprisingly Spain has some of the best almond dishes, including *sopa d'almendras*, almond soup. Other recipes omit the garnish of grapes but include instead a final sprinkling of cinnamon or rose petals. A beguiling touch, though one must concede that the counterpoint between the sweetness of the grapes and the pungency of the garlic is difficult to beat. Perhaps you could use both. The consistency is again a matter of taste.

I have eaten this soup in Spain where the almonds have been no more than roughly blended leaving large, crunchy pieces at the bottom of the soup. I prefer a smoother soup, with just a slight grittiness. You will, in any case, never get a really smooth cream. This is a soup which needs salt; it is entirely insipid without.

3½ oz / 100 g unblanched almonds; 2 juicy cloves of garlic; scant pint / 500 ml of water; 2 tablespoons of mild olive oil; ½–1 teaspoon salt; 1 dessertspoon wine vinegar. *To finish:* a few ice-cubes; a few sweet grapes, halved and pips removed.

Start with unblanched almonds. Peel them by pouring on boiling water and leaving them to steep for a minute or so. Take them out, one at a time, and the skins should rub off easily. Blend the first 4 ingredients to a smoothish cream. Add salt to taste, cover and chill for a couple of hours to allow the flavours to develop. Just before serving, add the wine vinegar. Ladle into delicate bowls or china fruit dishes, add a few grapes, a couple of ice-cubes and serve. A lovely soup to start a formal summer meal, or for eating out of doors on a languid summer's day.

ENGLISH ALMOND SOUP WITH HEDGEHOG ROLLS

This recipe, pared down to its essentials, is the 'white soop' of medieval England. Loved by whose who could afford it, it remained popular until well into the nineteenth century. Most modern versions are more faithful to the original recipes and call for egg yolks, a good quantity of cream and a butter and flour liaison to thicken the soup further. This is altogether a lighter affair.

1–1¼ pint / 600–750 ml chicken stock; 1 large stick of celery; 2 oz / 60 g ground almonds; milk; a little cream (optional).

Simmer the first 3 ingredients, uncovered, in a medium sized pan for about 25 minutes. Remove the celery. At this stage the soup looks rather unpromising but it will right itself shortly. Transfer to a liquidiser and blend at high speed until smooth and creamy. You will find that the soup lightens in colour and thickens slightly as the almonds become amalgamated with the stock. Return to the pan, add sufficient milk to dilute to a fairly thin consistency, a little swirl of cream if it's available, and serve – if the idea appeals – garnished with little hedgehog rolls. Make these as follows: cut ovals about 1¼ in / 3 cm long from thinly rolled puff pastry (trimmings are fine), one end pointed to resemble a snout. Stick with flaked almonds arranged in herring-bone fashion to represent spines, and bake in a hot oven for about 15 minutes.

FENNEL AND ALMOND SOUP

A useful recipe for using up the stalks and coarse, outer stems of fennel.

Soften 8–10 oz / 225–285 g of chopped fennel with a small chopped onion in a knob of butter in a covered pan. Add 2 oz / 60 g ground almonds and 1 pint / 600 ml of water or light chicken stock, cover, and simmer for 20–25 minutes until the fennel is cooked. Put through the medium blade of the *mouli*, or blend and then sieve to remove any stringy bits. Return to the pan, adjust the consistency with a little more water or milk, bring to the boil and serve, garnished with a little finely chopped fennel leaves and a spoonful of yoghurt.

BOUILLON MIT FRISCHEM MARK

This is undoubtedly one of the most elegant soups you could ever wish to find. We had it first in Germany and it took some time to realise that the delicious, small, opaque morsels were no more than slices of fresh beef marrow. It's such a simple idea, and so good.

1 pint / 600 ml consommé, clarified and of good flavour; slices of fresh beef marrow.

The success of the soup depends entirely on two things: the quality of the consommé, and the way you treat the marrow. A well-flavoured game stock, reduced further and clarified with egg whites in the usual way, is admirable, and this is what I generally use myself. Failing this, simmer some prepared beef stock with 4 oz / 120 g minced beef, a piece of pork rind and the usual vegetable flavourings until it is good and strong. Cool, strain off the fat and clarify.

Most recipes will tell you to poach marrow first but this is a mistake. It requires great skill and, unless properly done, most of it is lost, its richness dissolved for ever in the water. The slices must not be too thick or abundant. Part of the charm of this soup lies in having just the right number of these tasty morsels; too many and the marrow's distinctive richness soon becomes cloying. Fresh marrow bones are easily obtained and cost very little. Get the butcher to saw one into three, carefully prise out the marrow, and slice into rounds about $\frac{1}{4}$ in / $\frac{1}{2}$ cm thick. Allow 3 or 4 per person and set aside on a plate.

When you're ready to serve, bring the consommé to boiling point, ladle into heated soup cups or elegant bowls, add the slivers of marrow and serve immediately. An aristocrat among soups.

STRAWBERRY AND BASIL CONSOMMÉ
A soup with a heady quality and a 'twenties' feel, redolent of tennis parties and sweeping English lawns. Like all fruit soups, it's best served in restrained portions. Follow with something like trout, salmon, or a poached chicken, and a gooseberry fool or syllabub to finish.

1 lb / 450 g fresh ripe strawberries; 1–2 tablespoons sugar; approx. 2 glasses of reasonable red wine; 1–2 dessertspoons finely chopped basil; mineral water to dilute; ice-cubes.

Purée the strawberries, keeping a few to one side, and sieve to remove the pips if these are disagreeable to you. Dilute the purée with wine and water in the proportion of about 2:1 until it is the consistency of single cream. Be guided by your own taste. Add enough sugar to bring out the flavour of the fruit without making it too sweet. Add the reserved strawberries, chopped into bite-sized pieces. Chill until required. Just before serving, stir in finely chopped basil, cautiously, to taste. Ladle into soup cups, add an ice-cube, and serve immediately.

CRAB BISQUE
This soup may be more troublesome than most, but it's worth it. Made with left-over debris from a fresh crab, it produces a first-rate soup for next to nothing. Thoroughly recommended.

1 or more crab carcasses, including legs, and any prawn shells if available; 2 cloves of garlic, crushed; 2 oz / 60 g each of onion, leek, carrot and celery, all finely chopped; 2 tablespoons tomato purée; 2 fl oz / 60 ml brandy; small glass white wine; bouquet garni including small sprig of tarragon or basil; pinch of cayenne; 2 pints / generous litre water; knob of butter or 1 tablespoon olive oil for frying.

To finish: 2 tablespoons ground rice; milk; single cream; finely chopped chives, dillweed or chervil; extra crab meat (optional).

Begin with a whole crab, bought for another purpose. Break off the claws and the legs and scrub thoroughly. Now carefully and gently scrub the outside of the shell, not allowing too much water inside where the meat is. Open the crab up, remove the pointed flap, discard the mouth parts and the dead man's fingers and extract the meat in the usual way. Smash the claws and legs removing what meat you can without being too fussy. Keep back a tablespoon or so of white meat for the soup and use the rest for another dish. You are now ready to make the soup. If enthusiasm is waning, freeze all the debris for future use, checking that the inside skeleton is clean.

In a large pan melt a knob of butter or a tablespoon of olive oil – butter for the bisque, and oil for the broth (see below) – and gently sweat the vegetables for about 5 minutes until they soften. Keep the lid on and watch they don't catch. Add all the crab debris, and cook for a further 5 minutes or so. Pour on the brandy and the wine, let it bubble for a couple of minutes, then add the rest of the seasonings and water. Bring to the boil, skim, and simmer for 35–40 minutes. Fish out as many of the large pieces of shell as you can and strain the soup, sieving through as much of the debris as possible, including any meat that still remains attached to the inside shell. Taste and check the seasoning, making any final adjustments necessary. The soup is now ready. It's a thinnish, red-brown broth which can be served as it is, with croûtes spread with aïoli and maybe a little extra crab meat stirred in.

For a bisque-like version, return the broth to the pan, add 2 tablespoons of ground rice and simmer for a further 15 minutes. Dilute with enough milk to give the soup a creamy feel, stir in some extra crab meat, and serve with a swirl of cream and a sprinkling of fresh herbs.

GRATED CUCUMBER SOUP

Cucumbers make delightful soups. This one, adapted from an Elizabeth David recipe, is one of the best. A soup to fall back on when something refreshing yet substantial is called for, but when inspiration and time are wanting. Ridge cucumbers will need to be peeled first, others can be peeled or left unpeeled as you prefer.

6–8 oz / 170–225 g peeled and diced potato; medium onion, chopped; 1 whole cucumber; ½ small leek or two large spring onions; 1 teaspoon mint; 1 dessertspoon each of parsley and chives; small pickled gherkin (optional); 1 pint / 600 ml water; milk.

Boil the onions and potatoes in the water until cooked. Sieve or blend and dilute to a thin purée with milk. Grate the cucumber into the soup

and add the other ingredients, all finely chopped. Reheat cautiously,
check the seasoning and serve. [Serves 6.]

CUCUMBER AND WALNUT SOUP
A similar soup which calls for buttermilk, an underrated product, and
one whose name obscures its true nature. It is virtually fat free and has a
mild, pleasantly acidic taste. If not available, substitute thin yoghurt.
Quantities of ingredients can be varied to taste.

2–3 oz / 60–90 g walnuts, blanched in hot water to remove the skins;
1–2 cloves of garlic; scant tablespoon of olive oil; up to a whole
cucumber. To dilute: buttermilk or thin yoghurt; little sour cream or
single cream; water.

Begin by chopping the walnuts and garlic and then pounding them to a
smoothish paste with the olive oil in a pestle and mortar. Scrape into a
bowl and dilute with the buttermilk or yoghurt until there's enough for
four small servings, diluting if necessary with a little water. Add sour
cream or single cream to taste. Peel and chop the cucumber into the
tiniest of dice, stir into the soup, adjust the consistency with more liquid
if needed and chill until required. No garnishing is necessary, though I
find it difficult to resist a little finely chopped chives or dill, or a couple
of small, dainty mint leaves to set off the translucent quality of these
cool-looking soups.

CHINESE FISH AND CORIANDER SOUP
The Chinese view their meals differently from us, more as a harmonious
whole than a series of disparate elements. They have a way with soups,
especially the light and refreshing kind. This one is taken from *The
Complete Encyclopaedia of Chinese Cooking*. I have made one or two
minor changes and reduced the overall quantities slightly.

1 pint / 600 ml chicken stock; 6–8 oz / 170–225 g white fish e.g. whiting,
free from skin and bone; cornflour; lightly beaten egg white; ½ in / 1 cm
stick of fresh ginger cut into *julienne* strips; 1 tablespoon wine vinegar;
heaped tablespoon finely chopped coriander leaves; salt and pepper
(optional).

Cut the fish into bite size pieces, pat dry in kitchen paper and dip each
piece into cornflour. Shake off any excess. Reserve on a plate. Bring the
stock and slivers of ginger to the boil. With a fork, dip each piece of fish
into the egg white, transfer to the pan and poach until just tender, about

4–5 minutes. Add the vinegar, stir in the coriander, check the seasoning and serve.

BASIL AND TOMATO GAZPACHO

10 fl oz / 300 ml jellied chicken stock; 10 fl oz / 300 ml fresh tomato sauce or equivalent quantity of sieved canned tomatoes; 1 large clove of garlic, mashed to a pulp or finely chopped; handful of basil leaves, finely chopped and pounded to a paste; 1–2 teaspoons wine vinegar; 1–2 tablespoons olive oil.

Accompaniments: olive oil; chopped fresh tomatoes; chopped spring onions; diced cucumbers; diced red and green peppers; stoned black olives; garlic croûtons; ice-cubes.

Combine the first 4 ingredients. The base should be on the thin side so be prepared to dilute with a little iced water. Add seasoning and wine vinegar to taste – there should be just a hint of sharpness – and chill until required. Stir in 1–2 tablespoons olive oil and ladle into soup plates. Float a couple of ice-cubes in each portion and hand the accompaniments separately, together with extra olive oil.

The jellied stock adds an interesting texture to the soup and melts away as the soup is eaten. The garlic croûtons and ice-cubes are important, the stoned olives optional.

CURRIED PARSNIP SOUP

Jane Grigson made us realise the true potential of parsnips, one of our best winter vegetables, and her curried parsnip soup, which she first produced in 1969, has become a classic. This is a more everyday version: I have been known to eat it for weeks on end.

8 oz / 225 g diced parsnip; medium onion, chopped; crushed clove of garlic; 1 level dessertspoon each of curry powder and potato flour; 1¼ pint / 750 ml of lamb or beef stock, free from fat; extra milk; curry croûtons or a sprinkling of finely chopped coriander; ⅓–½ oz / 10–15 g butter.

Melt the butter and sweat the vegetables in a heavy, covered pan over a gentle heat for about 10 minutes. Stir in the curry powder and potato flour, cook for a minute, add the hot stock and cook until the parsnips are tender, about 20–30 minutes. Blend, return to the pan and dilute with a little milk until the soup is a consistency somewhere between thin and thick cream. This point is important; it's one of those soups where the consistency must be just right, neither too thick nor too thin. Bring to the boil and serve with a bowl of curry croûtons handed separately, or a sprinkling of finely chopped coriander.

Other variations worth trying are parsnip and apple, or parsnip and watercress. Make as before, substituting half the parsnip with peeled and chopped cooking apple and omitting the final thinning with milk; or add a handful of washed watercress to the vegetable mixture, leaving out the final garnish of coriander. Should stock not be available, use water. The soup will have less body but the taste will be cleaner. Both are very good.

HANNAH GLASSE'S PARTRIDGE SOUP

'Take two large old partridges, skin them and cut them into pieces with three or four slices of ham, a little celery, and three large onions cut in slices; fry them in butter till they are brown; be sure not to burn them; then put them to three quarts of boiling water, with a few peppercorns, and a little salt; stew it very gently for two hours, then strain it, and put some stewed celery and fried bread. Serve it up hot in a tureen.'

The Art of Cookery Made Plain and Easy, 1796

A handsome recipe which needs little explanation. It easily adapts to any game. Use any meaty carcass(es) with maybe an additional pigeon and proceed as follows.

Brown a large onion, 2 sticks of diced celery, 2 oz / 60 g diced bacon and the carcasses. As with any consommé, the success of the soup depends on this preliminary browning. Use a gentle heat and let everything sweat for up to half an hour or until the ingredients are beautifully browned without being burned. Give an occasional stir. Add 3–4 pints / a good 2 litres of water, 3–4 peppercorns, an unpeeled tomato, a piece of dried mushroom or a few mushroom stalks and a piece of pork rind if available. No salt. Bring to the boil, remove all the scum and simmer over the lowest possible heat until the stock is reduced by half or the broth is of a good flavour. Strain, remove any fat and reserve.

For each serving allow a tablespoon of celery, cut into tiny dice and cooked in a knob of butter until soft but still with bite. Pour on a ladleful of broth per person, bring to the boil and serve, handing round a bowl of croûtons separately.

Using previously prepared game stock from the freezer, this soup is but five minutes' work.

CONSTANCE SPRY'S COLD PEA SOUP WITH FRESH MINT

Constance Spry loved her vegetable garden as much as her flowers, and wrote about it with great enthusiasm and affection in her book, *Come into the Garden, Cook*, first published in 1942. Her recipes reflect the time – margarine instead of butter, a lack of cream, careful regard to eggs and milk 'if you can spare them'. For all their economy, they have an enduring charm. This is her pea soup, made from the pods.

'Take young fresh pea shells and cut off the stringy parts at top and bottom. Cut or break them up roughly, just so that the juice from them will run easily. Have ready a pan of boiling liquid, for choice the water in which the peas themselves have been cooked, or potato water, or plain water, or a mixture. Plunge the pods into this, add an onion and a few pieces of mint. When cooked put through a hair sieve. Return to the pan and reheat, season with salt and pepper and a touch of sugar and add as much milk as you like and can spare. If you have it, put a spoonful of cream in each cup, sprinkle very finely chopped mint on the surface, and chill well. This is fresher in taste, I think, than soup made from the peas themselves, and you can vary its richness by the amount of milk or cream you use. You can also vary the flavour by using other herbs instead of mint.'

For 1 lb / 450 g prepared pea pods, allow 1¼ pints / 750 ml liquid. When cooked, blend and sieve vigorously to extract all the pea mush. I prefer, also, to remove the mint before blending. It produces a thin soup of good, fresh flavour. I find diluting with milk unnecessary. Serve the soup in small bowls with a swirl of cream or yoghurt. Sugar snap peas can also be used.

'DRUNKEN' PRAWNS

An instant oriental soup, more elegant than most, and the colours – the pink of the prawns and the bright green of the watercress – are particularly appealing.

Per person: ladle of Chinese broth (see p. 34); 6 prawns or 2 large Dublin Bay prawns chopped into pieces; few sprigs of watercress; sherry; *julienne* strips of ginger.

Sprinkle the prawns with sherry and leave for at least half an hour. Cut a very thin slice of fresh ginger into the thinnest *julienne* strips possible and reserve. Wash the watercress and choose the small sprigs, keeping the others for another dish. Bring the broth to the boil, add the prawns and their juice and the watercress. Simmer for a minute to heat through, add the ginger and ladle into heated soup bowls. If you're lucky enough to find some uncooked, giant prawns, use those, adding the watercress when they're cooked.

EDOUARD DE POMIANE'S PUMPKIN SOUP

'If you are making pumpkin soup, buy a slice weighing about 1 lb. You will need 1½ pints of milk and 2 oz of rice as well.

'Peel the pumpkin and cut the flesh into small pieces. Put them into a saucepan with a tumblerful of water. Boil for about 15 minutes, then mash the pumpkin to a purée. Add the milk and bring it to the boil. Now pour in the rice and season with salt and pepper. Simmer for 25 minutes.

'At this moment the rice should be just cooked. Adjust the seasoning to your taste adding, if you like it, a pinch of caster sugar. *I* prefer a sprinkling of freshly-milled black pepper.'

Cooking with Pomiane, 1962

The soup comes out a beautiful canary yellow, speckled white from the grains of rice, with an unexpected hint of sweetness. Quantities should serve 4–6. A little finely chopped basil makes a good addition.

LADY CLARK'S SUMMER SOUP

A recipe from *Eat at Pleasure, Drink by Measure*, a collection of recipes compiled from leaflets sent over the years by Christopher's Wine Merchants to their customers. Elizabeth David was a regular contributor. This is one of hers, adapted from *The Cookery Book of Lady Clark of Tillypronie*, first published in 1909. It seems that Lady Clark's cook used crab or lobster left over from another dish, maybe as an afterthought, or maybe from thrift. Whatever the reason, it makes a lovely addition to a soup which Mrs David describes as a 'pleasing clear green with a good fresh flavour'. I use less butter and no salt, otherwise I follow her directions to the letter.

'Quantities for three ample helpings are: 1 oz butter, one leek, two sticks of celery including leaves, about ¼ lb each of green peas (shelled weight) and spinach, half a small fresh cucumber, seasoning, 1 pint of water, ¼ pint mild clear veal or chicken stock, a small quantity, say about two heaped tablespoons, of cooked crab or lobster meat.

'In a soup pot melt the butter. Put in first the cleaned and chopped leek together with the cucumber, unpeeled and coarsely grated, and the sliced celery. Add the peas and cleaned spinach. After ten minutes gentle cooking add 1 dessertspoonful of salt and a lump of sugar. Cook for another fifteen minutes. Sieve through the fine mesh of the *mouli* or reduce to a purée in the blender.

'Return this purée to the saucepan. Add the stock and the crab or lobster meat. Heat gently. Season with nutmeg.'

PERSIAN YOGHURT SOUP

The idea of yoghurt as a drink or a soup held little appeal for me until I was persuaded to try this recipe. It's a soup which has an immediate calming influence, very cool to look at, soothing to eat, and with all the freshness of summer. Accentuate its coolness by serving it in plain white dishes.

12 fl oz / 360 ml plain yoghurt; approx 5 fl oz / 150 ml water or light chicken stock; ½–1 medium onion, cut into paper-thin slices; at least half a grated cucumber; 1½–2 oz / 45–60 g black, seedless raisins; 2 hard-boiled eggs, finely chopped; finely chopped mint; 2 tablespoons thin cream (optional).

To finish: tiny mint leaves, crystallised violet flowers.

Pour boiling water over the raisins, leave to soak until nicely plump and then drain. Put the yoghurt into a bowl and beat in enough water or stock to give a fairly thin consistency but be guided by your own preference. Add the rest of the ingredients in the order given, mixing them in lightly. Use your discretion with the onion, not everyone's favourite seasoning. Adjust the consistency if necessary, add mint to taste and a swirl of cream if that seems a good idea, and chill until required. Just before serving, decorate each portion with tiny mint leaves and a crystallised violet if you have some.

Chopped dill and the white part of spring onions, finely sliced, can be substituted for mint and the stronger onion. A lovely variation.

Garden Things

Most people spoil garden things by over boiling them. All things that are green should have a little crispness, for if they are overboil'd they neither have any sweetness or beauty.

HANNAH GLASSE *The Art of Cookery Made Plain and Easy,* 1747

Nothing can compare with vegetables. At their best and in their prime, they require little in the way of embellishment. Cooked gently, with a knob of butter in a covered pan, most will cook in their own juices. The addition of a pat of savoury butter, a little chopped tomato or onion, or a sprig of basil or mint will make subtle changes without detracting from their fragile freshness. Older vegetables can be braised, stuffed or sauced with any number of savoury, spiced or herb mixtures. Fruit – particularly citrus fruit or dried fruit such as apricots and prunes – adds a welcome touch of sweetness. Vegetables combine well with pasta, rice and other cereals and they make splendid, economic stews with pulses, an excellent source of protein.

The potato is probably the most versatile vegetable of all. Theirs is an eventful but unhappy history. We have not been kind to our potatoes. We have classed them as poor man's food, good for nothing but filling you up and making you fat. At long last we are beginning to appreciate the enormous scope they offer and their nutritional worth. The value of raw fruit and vegetables is also gaining wide acceptance. Salads need not be smothered in mayonnaise or doused in oil and vinegar, a common fallacy which has for too long dominated our thinking and cookery books. Simpler dressings based on fruit juices or yoghurt provide excellent accompaniments and leave natural flavours unimpaired.

Cookery books always talk in ideal terms, particularly about vegetables. Sadly many are not the bright, fresh things we read about. Heavy with chemicals, they are all too often sickly specimens held too long in storage. To be sure of having the best, we must fall back on our own resources and grow our own. Once we had to dig for victory. Now, maybe, we need to dig for salvation.

Salads   *Personally, I would have a salad at every meal. I am told by people who know that salads are good for our health, that they contain vitamins or proteins or whatever it is. This is a poor inducement to our eating salads. The only true and human reason is that they are pleasant and useful.*

X. M. BOULESTIN *The Best of Boulestin*, 1951

A RAW BEGINNING

Not so long ago, raw vegetables were dismissed as rabbit food. Now, revamped as crudités, they're back in style. Aim to provide a selection of carefully chosen, fresh and neatly presented vegetables, elegantly cut into bite-sized pieces and arranged on a platter with various dips as accompaniments. They make a welcome splash of colour and a healthy, crisp start to a meal. Instead of the large bowl of mayonnaise customarily served in restaurants, go for something lighter, served in small bowls buried in the centre of the vegetable display.

A selection of raw vegetables, washed and sliced as appropriate: carrots, celery, sugar snap peas, mange-tout, radish, cucumber, fennel, peppers, celeriac, cauliflower etc.

Summer Dip
2 fl oz / 60 ml thick, sour cream; 2 fl oz / 60 ml thick, drained yoghurt; 1 oz / 30 g walnuts; 1 tablespoon finely chopped basil, sorrel or watercress.

Beat the yoghurt and the sour cream together and then lightly fold in the walnuts, chopped as finely as possible, and the herbs. Pile into a dish and serve chilled. [3–4 small servings.]

Arabian Dip
4 oz / 120 g cooked chick peas; up to 2 fl oz / 60 ml yoghurt; lemon juice; ground cumin; finely chopped mint; salt.

Blend the chick peas with enough yoghurt to give a smooth, thick purée. Transfer to a bowl and add the other seasonings to taste. A little tahini can also be added. Decorate with finely chopped mint and serve. See also Skordalia Cream, p. 53. [3–4 small servings.]

A CHOICE OF SALAD DRESSINGS

Thai-style dressing
I used to go occasionally to the Thai restaurant in Guildford and greatly liked their cucumber salad dressing. I was informed it was nothing more than vinegar, sugar and water. It's one of the best ideas I've come across, – light, sweetish and very refreshing. It can be used for all sorts of salads.

2 tablespoons wine vinegar, plain or flavoured; 2 tablespoons hot water; approx. 2 teaspoons sugar.

Simply mix the ingredients until the sugar has dissolved. It should be sweet but not over so. Made with basil or tarragon vinegar it makes a splendid dressing for cucumber salad and for winter salads based on shredded cabbage. With some added lime or lemon juice it's excellent for fish salads, avocado salads and those incorporating fresh fruit.

Fruit juice dressing for salade composée
Salades composées – mixed greenery arranged attractively on a plate – make stunning side-salads. They require little in terms of quantity so that, even allowing for something expensive like radicchio, the cost is low. They are especially useful in winter when good quality salad ingredients are scarce and expensive, yet something crisp and fresh is so welcome. Dressings based on fruit juice suit them particularly well.

2 tablespoons concentrated orange juice, such as that sold by Marks and Spencer; 1 tablespoon basil, tarragon or elderflower vinegar; 1 tablespoon walnut oil.

Arrange your salad on side plates as attractively as you can, choosing a selection from chicory, endive, radicchio, lamb's lettuce, watercress, strips of fennel, a few bean sprouts, hearts of lettuce. Mix together the salad dressing, spoon a little over each salad and serve.

Yoghurt and walnut dressing for green salads

For salad dressings I find walnut oil as useful as olive oil. It is expensive but you need very little. As well as its delicious flavour, it has the highest percentage of polyunsaturated oils (66%) of all nut oils.

Simply stir 1–2 dessertspoons of walnut oil into 2 fl oz / 60 ml of thick yoghurt until the oil is well amalgamated. Arrange a bed of crisp lettuce leaves on a plate, or four side plates if more appropriate, and spoon the dressing over to give a pretty patterned effect. The white is both striking and soothing. Decorate, if you like, with a few stoned and halved olives or some tiny garlic croûtes. A salad fit for a king.

Elderflower vinegar and honey dressing

For mixed winter salads. In a large bowl blend a teaspoon of honey with a tablespoon of elderflower vinegar. Add a tablespoon of oil of your choice – I generally use walnut – and beat until thick. Just before serving, pile the salad ingredients on top, toss, and arrange on side plates. If you include slices of orange in your salad, add any juices from the discarded pith and rind to the dressing.

Tomato vinaigrette

Good for watercress and spinach salads, for fish terrines, and for savoury mixtures encased in fila pastry.

For each smallish, very ripe tomato allow up to 2 tablespoons of olive oil and about a teaspoon of basil vinegar. Skin the tomatoes by pouring boiling water over them, extract the seeds saving any juice, and blend the chopped tomatoes with their juice and the olive oil in a blender or food processor until smooth. Stir in basil vinegar (or ordinary wine vinegar, if basil is not available) to taste, together with a pinch of sugar or a scrap of tomato purée if this seems necessary. Made in a blender, the vinaigrette is more rose-coloured than red. For a coarser and redder vinaigrette, reduce the tomatoes to a pulp by hand and then stir in the rest of the ingredients.

THE PERFECT LETTUCE SALAD

'Take from 6–8 cos lettuces, remove the outer and coarser leaves and strip from the remaining ones all the good part. The pieces should be 2½–3 inches long, and may be broken up but not cut.

Wash them and let them remain about half an hour in water, rinse in a second water, place them in a napkin and swing till dry.

For a dressing take the yolks of two hard-boiled eggs, crush them to a paste in a bowl, adding half a teaspoon of French vinegar, three mustard spoons of mustard, a salt spoonful of salt, and beat up well together; then add by degrees 6–8 tablespoons of Lucca or Provence oil and one of vinegar, and when thoroughly mixed add a little tarragon finely chopped and a dessertspoon of common white pepper. When all is well mixed place the salad in it, and turn it over thoroughly and patiently till there remains not one drop of liquid at the bottom of the bowl.

Put the whites of the eggs in slices on the top, and serve.'

MRS HILDA LEYEL *Green Salads and Fruit Salads, c.* 1935

LETTUCE SALAD WITH BUTTER AND ALMOND DRESSING

My own favourite lettuce salad. For lettuces of character – firm, green and sweet, rather than those poor, unfortunate things which have never known mother earth, felt the sun's rays or the early morning dew.

Select the best leaves from a green, crisp lettuce such as Tom Thumb, reserving the others for soups or to shred in salads. Wash and dry them carefully and arrange in a salad bowl. For a bowlful of lettuce leaves you need about 1 oz / 30 g of butter and 1–1½ oz / 30–45 g lightly toasted almond flakes. Melt the butter over a low heat with a crushed clove of garlic and let it infuse for a few minutes to absorb the flavour of the garlic. Then, very slowly and carefully, dribble the butter over the lettuce leaves, making sure that every leaf gets its drop of butter. Scatter the almonds over the top and serve immediately as a first course accompanied only by a few quarters of fresh orange.

HEATHER'S WET SALAD

'Wet salad' is a northern English invention. It's eaten as a side-salad with Yorkshire pudding and gravy and is, I suppose, a sort of glorified mint sauce with chopped lettuce. This version was given to me by a friend, a local farmer's wife and very good cook.

1 lettuce, preferably with the outer, coarser leaves removed; ½ small onion; 2 tablespoons chopped mint.

For the dressing: a little creamy milk; few drops of vinegar; ½–1 teaspoon sugar; salt and pepper (optional).

Finely chop together the lettuce, onion and mint and put the salad into a serving bowl. In a separate dish mix the dressing, adding vinegar and sugar to taste. Toss the salad in the dressing – there should just be enough to wet it nicely, and serve.

The result is both refreshing and piquant. I cannot say I share the traditional enthusiasm for wet salad and Yorkshire pudding, but as an accompaniment to cold meat salads or something like cracked wheat pilaff, I find it excellent. Heather also recommends it with a meal of grilled bacon, eggs and steamed new potatoes.

WINTER-SLAW

A healthier version of coleslaw, a dish I have never found particularly appealing. Use whatever salad ingredients are available, building them up in layers, and dress with Thai-style dressing (p. 49). Slight changes in ingredients produce enough variations on a theme to last the winter through.

Choose finely sliced cabbage as the base, either red, white or a mixture of the two, and place in the bottom of a salad bowl. Next add a layer of diced apple and celery, followed by a layer of greenery such as chopped lettuce, watercress, Chinese cabbage, thinly sliced sprouts, diced cucumber or a mixture of these. Follow, if you like, with another layer of cabbage and decorate the top with finely grated carrot and parsnip. These look most attractive arranged in mounds or as a border around the outside. Scatter with a few raisins and sesame or sunflower seeds. Add the dressing as you go along, leaving the top layer plain. A little diced tomato, banana or some chopped grapes can also be added.

NERO'S SALAD

A colourful red cabbage salad for winter. Good on its own, or with game.

For four people, take about 4–6 oz / 120–170 g red cabbage and a bunch of watercress; for the dressing, the juice of a lemon or half a grapefruit, including the flesh pressed through a sieve, a teaspoon of sugar and a tablespoon of olive oil.

Remove the hard core from the cabbage and, using a serrated knife, carefully shred it as thinly as you can. Cut it crossways into strips of about $2\frac{1}{2}$ in / 6.25 cm and put into a bowl. Pick the watercress over, wash, pat dry, pinch off all the best sprigs from the stalk and keep these to one side. Chop the remainder and add to the cabbage. Mix the dressing and toss the salad. Transfer to a shallow serving dish and decorate with the reserved sprigs of watercress.

RAW ENERGY SALAD

This is a simple and adaptable salad along the lines suggested by Leslie and Susannah Kenton in their stimulating book *Raw Energy*. It incorporates both fruit and vegetables, using whatever ingredients are available. With or without bread, it makes a substantial and easily-made lunch, light evening meal or packed lunch.

As available: white cabbage, carrot, celery, cucumber, tomato, radish, banana, apple, pear, few peeled and halved grapes, fresh peach or apricot, dried raisins or sultanas, orange juice to moisten, sprouted beans, yoghurt, a few chopped nuts, sunflower or sesame seeds.

The quantity of fruit and vegetables needed is small and they should be diced, sliced or shredded as appropriate. Avoid large chunks. Use only enough cabbage to provide the necessary bulk, and add other ingredients in proportion and to taste. Simply put everything into a bowl, mix lightly and moisten with a little orange juice. Transfer to serving dishes – large soup plates are ideal – top with yoghurt and serve.

   This is the basic mix. It can be varied according to the fruit and vegetables in season and to individual taste. A little finely sliced fennel, chopped watercress or grated raw beetroot make good additions.

CARROT AND PEPPER SALAD WITH
SKORDALIA CREAM

A summer salad for fresh, young carrots and crisp, shiny green peppers. The skordalia cream is a mild and creamy version of skordalia, the Greek equivalent of aïoli, but made with almonds instead of egg yolks. It has many uses as a dip for crudités and vegetable fritters, a sauce for fried or grilled fish, or with boiled potatoes, cooked beetroot and blanched french beans.

Skordalia Cream
2 oz / 60 g ground almonds; 2 fl oz / 60 ml olive oil; approx. 2½ fl oz / 75 ml hot water; 4 cloves garlic; slice of white bread from a small loaf; lemon juice or wine vinegar; salt (optional).

First prepare the sauce. Remove the crusts from the bread, soak briefly in water, squeeze out all the excess moisture and transfer to a small bowl or mortar. The bread serves to soften the sauce and fill it out. A little more will give a creamier sauce, a little less a grainier feel. About ½ oz /15 g, crusts removed, should be about right. Blanch the cloves of garlic in boiling water for 2–3 minutes, drain and mash to a pulp. Add the garlic to the bread and pound together to form a homogenous paste. Next add the almonds gradually, pounding well, adding a little hot water to soften the paste and make it easier to work. When thoroughly blended, add the oil, a little at a time as you would for mayonnaise, beating thoroughly after each addition. Again a few drops of hot water help. Finally add a little lemon juice, vinegar or both to sharpen, and stir in enough hot water to give a thick, smooth sauce which should not be runny but have a soft dropping consistency. Taste to check the seasoning, pile into a small bowl and set aside.

Skordalia Cream can also be made successfully in a food processor. Mash the garlic and blend in the processor with the bread paste, almonds, oil, and most of the hot water. Add extra hot water to give the desired consistency and leave the final seasonings to last.

To assemble the salad, cut the tops off the carrots, leaving ¼ in / 0.6 cm tuft of green. Scrub and cut in half vertically. Wash the peppers, take out the seeds and any pithy bits, and slice into even strips. Put the skordalia cream into the centre of a serving plate and arrange the carrots and peppers alternately in a circle around the sauce bowl keeping the pointed end of the carrots to the inside. Eat with your fingers, dipping the vegetables into the sauce.

CARROT AND RICE SALAD

Another beautiful salad and very easy. In summer serve it with plain, English-style salads or as part of a mixed *mezze* when eating out of doors; in winter, as a side-salad to accompany cracked wheat pilaff, savoury millet or cooked lentil dishes, or as a first course before the meat. This quantity will serve 4–6 depending on appetites and other elements in the meal.

1 lb / 450 g carrots, scrubbed and peeled; 2 tablespoons basmati rice; ⅓–½ oz / 10–15 g butter; water; finely chopped mint or chervil (optional).

For the dressing: 1 tablespoon sunflower or other vegetable oil; 2 tablespoons lemon juice; scant teaspoon honey.

Cut the prepared carrots into neat *julienne* strips and sweat in a good knob of butter for 3–4 minutes. Add the rice, stir it round to coat with the juices from the carrots, and moisten with a few tablespoons of water, just enough to create some steam and to prevent the vegetables from sticking or catching. Cover, bring to the boil and cook hard for 2 minutes. Remove from the heat and leave to sit. The vegetables and rice continue to cook as they cool.

Mix the dressing and pour over the salad, turning the carrots and rice over to coat well. There should only be enough to moisten the vegetables. Transfer to a serving dish and serve at room temperature, plain or sprinkled with a dusting of finely chopped mint or chervil.

This is an excellent way of cooking carrots to serve as a hot vegetable. After the preliminary boiling, leave them for 10–15 minutes and serve them hot, without the dressing.

CELERIAC AND LEMON SALAD

In the *Alice B. Toklas Cook Book*, Ms Toklas gives a recipe for lemon salad, passed on to her by her friend Dr Fernanda Pivano-Sottsass from Milan. The lemons are boiled to softness, diced and added to artichoke hearts and almonds, the whole mixed with a dressing of lemon juice, olive oil and honey. An intriguing idea; the lemons impart a sharp tang which, used with discretion, can profitably be employed to liven up many salads.

Boil a scrubbed lemon in gently boiling salted water until soft and yielding but not yet burst. This will take about 45 minutes, but the time varies from lemon to lemon. Drain, cool, cut into tiny neat dice, discarding the pips, and set aside. Prepare about 8 oz / 225 g celeriac, cutting it into *julienne* strips approximately the size of thin chips. Blanch in boiling water for 2 minutes. They should be just cooked, so allow a little more or less time accordingly. Drain, refresh and pat dry. Add the diced lemon to the celeriac, enough to give a pronounced tang without being overbearing – I find half the lemon is about right but it's very much a question of personal taste. Mix the two lightly but thoroughly. Blend 2–3 tablespoons of mayonnaise with an equal quantity of hot water or milk and toss the salad in the dressing. Transfer to individual dishes, garnish with a little finely chopped parsley or chives and serve. Sit the salad in a border of lettuce leaves if you have them.

SORREL OR TARRAGON EGG MAYONNAISE

Egg mayonnaise, cholesterol aside, is calorie-wise a weighty thing but, by the simple expedient of thinning down some good mayonnaise, and coating the eggs a little more lightly, such pitfalls can be avoided.

For the mayonnaise: 1 large or 2 small fresh egg yolks; approx. ¼ pint / 150 ml oil; good pinch of salt; lemon juice or wine vinegar; ½ teaspoon of mustard (optional); 1–2 tablespoons finely chopped sorrel or tarragon.

Blenders and food processors make excellent, fool-proof mayonnaise in next to no time. Substitute one whole egg for the egg yolk, or use one whole egg and one egg yolk for a larger quantity. One whole egg will absorb up to ⅓ pint / 200 ml oil, and may take more. Put the egg(s) into the warmed blender bowl together with a little lemon juice or vinegar and mustard, if used. Salt too. Blend for a few seconds and then start adding the oil gradually while the motor is running. Continue until the mayonnaise is as thick and creamy as you want. The whole process should not take more than a couple of minutes. Taste and make any adjustments to seasoning as necessary.

There is pleasure to be derived from making mayonnaise by hand, great satisfaction in watching eggs and oil amalgamate, as if by magic, under the slow, rhythmic beat of a wooden spoon. There's no need to feel apprehensive. As long as both eggs and oil are at room temperature, and you are patient in the early stages, mayonnaise is unlikely to curdle. Should it do so, a tablespoon of boiling water usually brings it back. If this fails, start again with a fresh egg yolk, gradually incorporating the curdled mayonnaise before adding any more oil.

The choice of oil is crucial as mayonnaise always accentuates its flavour. It is a question of personal taste. Except for aïoli, which does insist on your best, fruity olive oil, a blend of oils, such as one part or less of olive oil and two parts of a mixture of ground nut or grape seed and safflower oil produces satisfactory results. Seasonings too are a matter of taste, though a little mustard helps to emulsify the egg and makes it easier to incorporate the oil.

To make the mayonnaise, beat the egg yolk with the salt and mustard, if used, until thoroughly mixed. Add the oil, drop by drop to begin with, and then – but still with caution – in a slow, steady stream as the mixture thickens. Add a few drops of lemon juice, vinegar, or both as you go along. Taste and make any final adjustments to seasoning. One large egg yolk will easily absorb up to ¼ pt / 150 ml oil though I tend to stop when the mayonnaise is as thick as I want and the taste seems right.

For sorrel or tarragon mayonnaise, remove the mid-ribs from the sorrel and the tarragon leaves from its stalk, chop and then pound almost to a purée in a wooden mortar. This produces a finer and altogether more pleasing, herbed mayonnaise, lightly speckled and with an attractive greenish hue which simply stirring chopped herbs into the mayonnaise does not achieve. Incorporate a tablespoon of mayonnaise into the herb purée and then blend in sufficient mayonnaise to meet your requirements. Set aside.

To assemble the salad, lay the halved eggs, white side uppermost on a white, handsome serving dish. Take about 1–2 tablespoons of herbed mayonnaise per person and let it down gradually, a teaspoon at a time, with some hot water until the mixture is somewhere between thin and thick cream in consistency. It should not be too runny but should spread a little. Coat the eggs with the mayonnaise and serve. As decoration, a few single tarragon leaves or tiny fronds of sorrel can be used to good effect, but be careful not to detract from the cool, summery beauty of the finished dish.

TWO FRENCH BEAN SALADS
French beans have invaded our shops and our gardens with a determination that Napoleon would be proud of. Given time, they'll probably oust peas as our favourite vegetable. Should we mind? They are prolific and adaptable. Unlike most vegetables whose peak of perfection lasts but a short time, french beans are good to eat whatever their age. Here are two salads for the very young. Elsewhere in this chapter you will find recipes for their older brothers and sisters.

French Beans with Walnut Dressing
Top and tail some young french beans, pencil slim if you can get them, and blanch them for 1–2 minutes in a large pan of boiling water, keeping them decidedly *al dente*. Drain and set aside on kitchen paper to soak up any remaining moisture. With such a short cooking time they will keep their bright green colour. Toss them in a little walnut oil to which you have added a tablespoon or so of finely chopped walnuts. Arrange neatly on a plate and serve, preferably while still tepid but, in any event, not chilled. Please do not be put off by the complete simplicity of this dish. The combination really is very good.

French Beans with Yoghurt and Cinnamon Dressing
Blanch the beans (as in the previous recipe) and pat them dry in kitchen paper. Arrange them in a neat line along the length of a pretty oval plate, stacking them in rows on top of each other. Mix together some plain yoghurt with a little powdered cinnamon – about a teaspoon per ¼ pint / 150 ml yoghurt – and a pinch of sugar. Spoon some of the dressing down the centre of the beans and serve the rest separately. Blanched broccoli florets can be prepared in the same way.

GREEK SALAD
My favourite salad.

Per person: 2 or more large sweet tomatoes; good 3 in / 7.5 cm stick of cucumber, peeled and thickly sliced; 1–1½ oz / 30–45 g Feta cheese; a few black olives, stoned and halved; good, fruity olive oil; lemon juice; chopped fresh oregano or dried rigani.

Use soup plates for this salad and arrange it Greek-style, individually, rather than in one large dish. An hour or so before you want to eat, chop a healthy quantity of fresh oregano and leave it spread out on a board. By the time you come to make the salad it will have almost dried, yet have all the flavour of the fresh herb. Start with the cucumber and lay the slices in the bottom of the plate, slightly overlapping each other. Ridge cucumbers are the best. Lay the sliced tomatoes on top of the cucumber in the same manner. Rather than crumble the Feta cheese, slice it into thin slivers and lay over the tomatoes. Scatter over the olives and the oregano – be liberal with the fresh herbs, more cautious with the dried – and dribble a little olive oil over the whole. Finish with a few drops of lemon juice and serve with pitta bread.

Fresh oregano is rarely available but golden marjoram (*Origanum vulgare aureum*) is an excellent substitute and worth growing.

EGG AND TOMATO SALAD
Carefully arrange alternate slices of hard-boiled eggs and tomatoes in a circular fashion on a plate. Roll up 3 or 4 of your largest basil leaves and, holding them over the salad, snip them very finely with a pair of kitchen scissors. Dribble over a little olive oil, decorate with one or more black olives and serve with pitta bread.

SWEET AND SOUR LEEK SALAD
Sweet and sour combinations were common in English cooking right up to the early nineteenth century. These days we tend to associate them more with oriental cooking. It's a pity we don't make more use of them. The results, strangely enough, are neither sweet nor sour but refreshingly piquant. This dish is based on an idea from Claudia Roden.

1½ lb / 675 g leeks; 1–2 cloves of garlic, crushed and chopped; 1 dessertspoon sugar; 2 tablespoons raisins; 2 tablespoons vegetable oil; juice of one large lemon; shavings of lemon rind; extra lemon juice.

Clean the leeks thoroughly and remove any outer tough stems and most of the green part. Slice fairly finely and set aside. Heat the vegetable oil and the sugar until the sugar turns light brown and begins to caramelise. Remove from the heat and let it cool a little. Add the leeks and the garlic. Turn them over to coat them in the oil and cook for a minute or two until they begin to soften. Add the juice of one lemon, cover, and cook gently for about 20 minutes until the leeks are tender. Taste, add extra lemon juice if necessary and stir in the raisins. Leave to cool. To serve, transfer to a shallow dish and sprinkle with a few tiny shavings of lemon rind.

HOT SALADS

A simple salad of lettuce leaves, dressed with the hot juices from meat, is acknowledged to be one of the finest dishes in the world. Lettuce used to mop up gravy or the sauce from a casserole is equally delicious. How well I remember as a child wrapping lettuce around mashed potato as you would a chappati around vegetables. Even then, it seemed one of the best ways to eat both lettuce and potato.

It's the contrast between hot and cold which makes these salads special. They're simply made: use any of the ingredients either singly or in a combination as you would for a green salad, arrange neatly on small plates and set aside. Next devise a savoury concoction to be cooked briefly and spooned over. The salad is now ready to be served, immediately, as a first course. Combinations which work best are those which include strips of meat such as frizzled bacon or lightly sautéed liver, and seasonings such as spring onions, mushrooms, olives, and fruit rather than those which contain a lot of different ingredients. Hot croûtons provide a crunchy contrast. The many possibilities soon become apparent.

HOT SALAD WITH CHICKEN LIVERS

8 oz / 225 g chicken livers; juice of 1 orange; 2 tablespoons chopped spring onion; 2 tablespoons fine *julienne* strips of carrot; 2–3 tablespoons Marsala; butter and oil for frying.

For the base: lettuce leaves, or endive plus a few sprigs of watercress, or raw, young spinach leaves.

If you have time, soak the chicken livers in milk for a couple of hours prior to making the salad. Drain, pat dry, remove any stringy or green looking bits, slice into sizeable pieces and set aside. Arrange the greenery on four plates, sprinkle with orange juice, scatter over the carrot and set aside.

Fry the spring onion in a little butter and oil for 2–3 minutes in a smallish pan. Turn up the heat, add a little more butter and oil if necessary, tip in the chicken livers and cook briskly, constantly turning and shaking the pan for a further 2–3 minutes. The livers should then be nicely pink inside. Add the Marsala, bubble up for a minute, spoon over the salads, and serve immediately.

HOT TONGUE (OR GAME) AND CAPER SALAD

6–8 oz / 170–225 g tongue, left-over game, or a mixture of both; 2 tablespoons vinegar; 1 tablespoon sugar; juice of 1 Seville orange or ½ sweet orange and ½ lemon; 1 tablespoon capers; 1 tablespoon raisins; a knob of butter and a little oil; salad greens.

Make a caramel with the vinegar and sugar by setting both over a moderate heat in a small pan. Stir until the sugar has dissolved and then cook until it turns to a golden brown caramel. Take off the heat immediately, let it cool somewhat and add the fruit juice. Do this an hour or so before you want the salad to allow the caramel to dissolve in the fruit juice. If any remains in the bottom of the pan, reheat gently.

To assemble the salad, arrange the salad greens on four plates. Cut the meat into strips and fry in a knob of butter and a little oil for 3–4 minutes until the edges are beginning to brown, stirring constantly. You will need to be careful with tongue for it tends to disintegrate and, although delicious, looks unappealing. Add the raisins and continue cooking for another minute or so until they've plumped up. Add the capers, pour over the heated orange caramel mixture, bubble up, spoon over the salads and serve immediately.

CHINESE HOT SALAD
WITH EGGS AND MUSHROOMS

Lettuce; 2 eggs, beaten; 8 oz / 225 g mushrooms, cleaned and sliced; 3–4 spring onions or white part of 1 leek, cut into *julienne* strips; vegetable oil for frying.

For the sauce: 2 tablespoons soy sauce; 2 tablespoons sherry; 1 teaspoon chilli sauce; 1 teaspoon sugar.

To finish: few drops of sesame seed oil.

Prepare four plates of lettuce leaves and set aside. Mix all the sauce ingredients and set aside, and have everything else at the ready. Make 4 thin, flat omelettes, cooking both sides as you would a pancake. Roll up and cut into thin strips. Heat 2–3 tablespoons of vegetable oil in a wok or large pan. Add the mushrooms and stir-fry for 30 seconds. Follow with the spring onion or leek and omelette strips and stir-fry for another 30 seconds, keeping the heat fairly high. Add the sauce ingredients, cook for a minute and spoon over the waiting beds of lettuce. Sprinkle each, very sparingly, with a few drops of sesame seed oil and serve immediately.

FLOWERS IN SALADS

'And why do we make so little use of flowers in salads? Rose petals, Nasturtiums, Sage flowers, Bergamot, Anchusa, Borage, Marigolds, Rosemary, and Lavender are some of the best edible flowers. It is a pity to waste Rose petals when they are going to drop, for they are particularly wholesome. Marigold petals too have very health-giving properties. The idea of eating flowers is disliked by some people, yet they do no hesitate to wear flowers and use flower essences for scents, etc., and I can see no real difference. Personally, I would rather eat a few flower petals than wear flowers and see them die slowly. Flower petals strewn in a mixture over a salad make it look very gay, and for a change try chopping finely a few tablespoons of mixed petals. It gives a salad a carnival look.'

ELEANOUR SINCLAIR ROHDE *Culinary and Salad Herbs*, 1940

SALADS USING FRUIT

I'm always surprised not to come across recipes for salads using fruit more often. Their clean, sweet refreshing qualities are as welcome at the beginning of a meal as at the end. Previous generations did not share our inhibitions; Mrs Leyel, for example, gave them frequently – a cherry salad with roast lamb, prune salad with grouse and the salad chosen here, Monte Carlo salad, with a cold mousse of rabbit.

Monte Carlo Salad

'Cut up some bananas and tomatoes neatly, and mix them with some grapes. Pour over them a mayonnaise to which has been added a dessertspoonful of anchovy essence and a little whipped cream.' The combination of tomatoes and bananas is unexpectedly delicious. Use approximately equal quantities of each, rather less of diced grapes, and go easy on the anchovy essence – tastes change over the years, and a hint is all that we require. Lightening the mayonnaise with yoghurt adds a faint sharpness, which sets off the sweetness of the fruit, which I find agreeable, but others may prefer Mrs Leyel's touch. Set the salad in a frill of lettuce leaves and serve as a first course.

Two Pear Salad

For each person allow half an avocado and half a ripe dessert pear of quality, such as a Williams or Doyenne du Comice. Peel and slice the fruit fairly thinly, dip into your chosen dressing, and arrange prettily on small plates. The attraction of this salad is the contrast in taste and texture between the smooth, velvety avocado and the sweet, juicy, slightly grainy texture of the pear, so overlap them in some way – it will give a most beautiful striped effect.

Mix together the juice of a lemon or a lime with a tablespoon each of wine vinegar and gin, vodka or Bacardi. Add 1–2 teaspoons of sugar and 1–2 tablespoons of hot water. Stir until the sugar has dissolved and spoon over the salad, decorating, if you like, with a few shavings of thinly pared rind.

Orange, Radish and Basil Salad

Prepare a couple of juicy oranges, cutting away the pith and peel and freeing the segments from membrane and pips. Reserve any juice and arrange in a star-like fashion on 4 small plates or in small fruit dishes. Crisp a few radishes in water, slice thinly, and arrange neatly in between the orange slices. Take 2 tablespoons of the reserved juice, add a dash of wine vinegar to sharpen, an equal quantity of olive oil, mix thoroughly, and spoon over the salad. Scatter the top with a liberal amount of finely shredded basil and chill before serving.

Salade Véronique

From Escoffier's *Ma Cuisine*. The quantities are mine.

4 oz / 120 g grapes, peeled and seeded; 2 slices of fresh pineapple, diced into neat cubes; 2–3 oz / 60–90 g chopped walnuts; 2 oranges; lettuce leaves taken from the heart.

For the dressing: 3–5 fl oz / 90–150 ml single cream; lemon and orange juice.

Prepare the oranges as in the previous recipe, reserving any juice. Dilute the cream with a little of the citrus juices in the proportion of one part citrus juice to three parts cream. Mix the fruit and walnuts, bind lightly with a little of the dressing. Arrange on lettuce leaves and serve the rest of the dressing separately.

Vegetables   Q. *'How do you boil peas ?'*
A. 'Briskly, ma'am.'

Finchley Manual for the Training of Servants, 1800

SUMMER MEDLEY

Prepare a roughly equal quantity (by volume) of shelled, baby broad beans and baby courgettes, scoring the skin of the courgettes with a canelle knife and slicing them into $\frac{1}{4}$ in / $\frac{1}{2}$ cm rounds. Scrub some baby carrots and cut them into thickish *julienne* strips allowing, say, half the volume of carrots to the other vegetables. Have a couple of sprigs of mint, a teaspoon or so of sugar, 1–2 tablespoons of raisins, and a little lemon juice at hand. Melt a good knob of butter in a heavy pan. Add the vegetables, sprinkle with sugar, tuck in the mint and cook gently, covered, for 4–5 minutes, shaking the pan occasionally. If you want crunchy carrots, add these towards the end. Scatter over the raisins and continue to cook until the vegetables are just tender. This should only take 3–4 minutes more, but will depend on your vegetables and their thickness. There should be enough moisture for the vegetables to cook in their own juices but if necessary add a tablespoon or so of water with the raisins. Remove the mint, sprinkle with a few drops of lemon juice, and serve.

BROAD BEANS WITH BACON AND SORREL

A simple and well-known dish but one that responds to a little extra care. The sorrel lifts it and adds a touch of distinction. Arrange the cooking so that the beans and bacon are ready together.

Cut a couple of slices, a good $\frac{1}{4}$ in / $\frac{1}{2}$ cm thick, from a piece of good quality streaky bacon. Take off the rind and cut each slice into thin strips, again about $\frac{1}{4}$ in / $\frac{1}{2}$ cm thick, so that you end up with a neat bundle of elongated cubes.

Put the bacon cubes in a dry, smallish pan and fry gently for 15–20 minutes until nicely crisp and most of the fat has come out. Set aside. Prepare the sorrel and beans as follows. Remove the central stalk from a handful of sorrel leaves and shred them finely. Bring a large pan of water to the boil and add about 1 lb / 450 g shelled broad beans. Bring back to the boil and cook over a brisk heat until the beans are tender – about 3 minutes from the time the water comes back to the boil. Drain and transfer to a dish. Add the bacon and its fat, mix well and scatter the sorrel over the top. The heat of the beans will soften the sorrel which provides a pleasing acidity to balance the saltiness of the bacon. Serve immediately, as a first course, in small heated dishes.

Removing the outside skins of the beans makes for a prettier dish, but I am in two minds over this. I like the skins and the fibre they provide, but the choice is yours.

SCANDINAVIAN BEETROOT

Boiled baby beetroot dressed with raspberry vinegar are a delight. But for older beetroot something more robust is required. Apples and onions go well and temper the earthy flavour of the beetroot with a little added sweetness and piquancy reminiscent of those braised red cabbage dishes which are so good in wintertime. This, too, is a winter dish, good with pork or sausages or as a vegetable dish in its own right.

8 oz / 225 g cooked beetroot, peeled and diced; 1 lb / 450 g cooking apples, peeled, cored and sliced; 1 medium onion, finely sliced; butter; finely chopped chives or parsley.

Soften the onion in a knob of butter in a covered pan. Add the beetroot and the apple and continue to cook gently, covered, for about 30 minutes until the apples and onion have formed a thick purée. The beetroot remains intact and the whole dish takes on a brilliant hue. Add a dusting of finely chopped chives or parsley and serve. The dish reheats very successfully.

SAVOURY CABBAGE

Half a savoy cabbage, shredded; 1 shallot, or half a small onion; 1 slice of lean bacon cut into tiny strips; chicken stock to moisten; 1–2 tablespoons vegetable oil and knob of butter for frying.

Choose a large frying pan with a lid, or use a wok. Gently sweat the onion until soft. Add the bacon, raise the heat slightly and cook until both bacon and onions are beginning to brown. Distribute the cabbage on top and pour in enough stock to cover the base of the pan and to prevent the cabbage from burning. You should not need more than a small glass full. Cover, turn up the heat and cook briskly for 2–3 minutes until the cabbage begins to wilt and give up its juices. Remove the lid and continue to cook over a high heat to evaporate the juices, another minute or so. Stir the cabbage around to distribute the bacon and onion and serve immediately. Excellent as part of a vegetable meal, or with pork or sausages.

STUFFED CABBAGE ROLLS

'If stuffed cabbage sounds downright dull,' wrote Shona Crawford Poole in her *Times* cookery column, 'read on because this version isn't'. She went on to describe a promising filling and a novel way of forming neat little cabbage cushions by twisting the filled leaves in a square of muslin. The rolls were recommended as a garnish for game or, with a sour cream and paprika sauce, as a meal in themselves. I have slightly amended her recipe.

12 large and 12 smaller leaves from a hard cabbage; 6 oz / 170 g cooked brown rice; 4 oz / 120 g cooked whole brown or green lentils; 2 oz / 60 g coarsely chopped walnuts; 1 oz / 30 g raisins; 1 small leek, finely chopped; 1 medium onion, finely chopped; 6 juniper berries, crushed and chopped; ½ teaspoon caraway seeds; 1 tablespoon olive oil; salt and pepper (optional).

For the sauce: medium onion, finely chopped; 12 oz / 340 g peeled tomatoes, tinned or fresh; 1 tablespoon paprika; 1 tablespoon chopped dill; 3–5 fl oz / 90–150 ml sour cream or thick yoghurt; knob of butter.

Blanch the cabbage leaves for 2 minutes in boiling water, drain, and pat dry. Remove the central rib with a Y-shaped cut towards the centre of each leaf. Gently sweat the onion and leek in the olive oil for about 5 minutes until soft and just beginning to brown. Remove from the heat and stir in all the other ingredients and mix thoroughly. To assemble the cabbage parcels take a large cabbage leaf, curly side up, and place it on a square of dampened muslin about 12 in / 30 cm square. Put a small leaf, same way up, in the centre of the large leaf and in the middle place a heaped tablespoon of stuffing. Fold the leaves loosely over the stuffing, gather up the corners of the cloth and twist tightly, squeezing the cabbage into a neat ball. Fill all the cabbage leaves in the same way. Arrange, join side down, in a steamer – Chinese baskets are ideal – and steam for about 15–20 minutes.

To make the sauce soften the onion in the butter without letting it brown. Off the heat stir in the paprika followed by the chopped tomatoes and dill. Simmer for about 15 minutes, blend or process and finish with sour cream or yoghurt to taste. To serve, pour the sauce into a heated serving dish and arrange the cabbage rolls in a single layer on top.

This quantity will amply feed 4–6 as a vegetable, allowing 1 to 2 each. As a main course allow 3 or 4 per person and serve with other vegetables such as green beans, broccoli or carrots. The filling makes an excellent dish in its own right, either hot or cold as a salad surrounded by a bed of lettuce leaves and sprinkled with a few finely chopped herbs.

STRAWED CARROTS

One of the best and easiest ways of cooking carrots. Coarsely grate as much carrot as you need – grated vegetables bulk up alarmingly and are best judged by eye rather than weight. Melt a knob of butter in a heavy pan, add the carrots and cook gently, turning them often, for 3–5 minutes until they soften and begin to exude their juices. They are now ready. Serve in the same pan or alternatively turn out on to a heated serving dish mounding them up attractively and decorating with tiny sprigs of chervil. Delicious.

GREEN-SPECKLED CAULIFLOWER

A nice summer dish to accompany meat, an omelette, or on its own.

1 cauliflower, divided into small florets; clove of garlic; generous tablespoon of chopped basil, tarragon, mint and parsley; 1 heaped tablespoon of fine dried breadcrumbs; 2–4 stoned and quartered black olives (optional); olive oil and butter for frying.

Chop the herbs and the garlic extremely finely using parsley to provide the bulk and a little of each of the others to add fragrance and piquancy. Set aside. Prepare the breadcrumbs; there should be about an equal volume of bread and herbs. Blanch the cauliflower florets in a large pan of boiling water for a minute only. Drain and transfer to a plate. In a shallow pan warm enough olive oil (1–2 tablespoons) to cover the base, add a knob of butter and let that melt also. Add the herb mixture and cook gently for a minute or so stirring it round with a wooden spoon; it shouldn't cook quickly and only just enough to soften the garlic slightly and release its aroma. Stir in the breadcrumbs to make a thick paste. Add the cauliflower, turning the florets over so that they become encrusted with the paste. Cook for another couple of minutes until everything is thoroughly hot, adding the olives, if used, at the end. Serve immediately in the same pan.

CAULIFLOWER STEAMED WITH BAY LEAVES

A tip picked up years ago from a cookery course run by the local W.I. When cooking cauliflower, add a couple of bay leaves, broken in half. The cauliflower absorbs their perfume and takes on some of their flavour. Useful for cauliflowers which aren't all they might be.

CELERIAC AND WALNUT PATTIES

Celeriac and walnuts both have strong, positive flavours which marry well together. These patties are good as part of a vegetable meal with, for example, sprouts, leeks or carrots and a bulgur pilaff.

1 lb / 450 g prepared celeriac, cut into even slices; 2 oz / 60 g walnuts; approx. 2 tablespoons potato flour; 1 dessertspoon each of finely chopped parsley and chervil; beaten egg; flour for coating; vegetable oil for frying.

Cook the celeriac in a covered pan with 1 in / 2.5 cm boiling water until soft. Drain and reserve. Grind the nuts finely in a blender or food processor. Add the celeriac and process again, for a few seconds only, until you get a rough paste with small but discernible lumps of celeriac in it. Transfer to a bowl and beat in the herbs, potato flour and enough egg to bind the mixture together. It should be soft but not sloppy. Divide into 8 equal portions, shape into flattish, round patties, and keep until required.

Just before cooking them, coat both sides in flour, patting off the excess with your fingers. Fry in shallow oil, turning once, for about 10–15 minutes until the outsides are nicely browned and crisp, the insides creamy and soft. Drain on absorbent paper and serve.

Chestnuts, How to Shell

'Every cook knows how tedious it is to shell any considerable quantity of chestnuts. The following plan is, therefore, of much interest. Cut a slit on the flat side of each chestnut. Put the chestnuts in a frying pan with a few dabs of butter. Heat the pan and shake all the while to get the nuts thoroughly greased. Then take them out of the pan; put them in an oven for 10 minutes and it will be found that the shells will almost come away by themselves.'

Success Cookery Book, 1500 New Economy Cookery and Household Recipes, 1932

A useful tip. Transfer the pan – no need to take the chestnuts out – to a hot oven. After a further 20 minutes or so they should be cooked through. Any fat or oil can be used.

CHESTNUT CROQUETTES

An easy recipe which sets off the natural creaminess of chestnuts. It is delicious with roast game or as part of a winter vegetable meal.

1 lb / 450 g chestnuts; 2 slices of lean boiled ham; single cream or creamy milk; fine dry brown or white breadcrumbs; vegetable oil.

Cook the chestnuts in boiling water for about 30 minutes or until the insides are soft. When cool enough to handle, cut them in half and scoop out the insides into a bowl. You should get a good 8 oz / 225 g of shelled cooked weight. This can be done in advance. Chop the ham finely or briefly process in a food processor. Add to the chestnuts and mash the two together with a fork and enough liquid to form a fairly stiff but creamy paste. Divide the mixture into even portions and shape into croquettes. I make mine about 2 × 1 in / 5 × 2.5 cm and this gives me approximately 9–10 from this amount of mixture, but you can make them larger or fatter as you wish. Roll each croquette in breadcrumbs and leave spread out on a plate for an hour or so to allow the breadcrumbs to set. When the time comes to cook the croquettes, heat a little vegetable oil in a large shallow pan and gently fry them for about 10 minutes, turning them frequently till evenly browned on all sides. Drain briefly on kitchen paper and serve garnished with a few sprigs of parsley.

COURGETTES WITH CINNAMON AND OREGANO BUTTER

Savoury butters are a must; they are easy to prepare, freeze well and are useful when you want to add that little something without preparing a sauce or doing anything elaborate. The permutations are endless – tarragon butter with tomatoes; orange butter with broccoli; sage and lemon with carrots and this, Russian fashion, for courgettes or baby marrows. A couple of pats is all that's required.

For 2 oz / 60 g butter allow about a dessertspoonful of finely chopped oregano and a scant teaspoon of cinnamon. Soften the butter, beat in the herbs and seasonings, and roll in butter paper to form a tube about 1 in / 2.5 cm thick. Chill in the refrigerator, or freezer if you're short of time, until very hard. Slice into $\frac{1}{4}$ in / $\frac{1}{2}$ cm pats and use as required. This quantity makes about 8 pats.

Slice the courgettes and cook in a knob of plain butter in a covered pan. For every 8 oz /225 g cooked vegetables add a couple of pats of savoury butter. Shake the pan to distribute the butter evenly and serve.

FENNEL THE ITALIAN WAY

A lovely vegetable, compared by Jane Grigson to 'celery that has been pressed down into bulbousness by a giant hand', highly aromatic, with an unmistakable, assertive taste of aniseed and a clean, crisp texture. It is best appreciated on its own. This is a simple recipe but worthy of the best fennel you can find.

Take off the outer layers which can be stringy, keeping them for soups and stocks (see p. 38), and cut the rest into fine strips. I suspect that price may determine how much you want to use, so quantities will be left to your discretion. Sweat the prepared strips in a knob of butter in a heavy pan which will just hold them comfortably. They will soften in about 5 minutes. Add enough concentrated and well-flavoured chicken or game stock to moisten. Allow to bubble up, take off the heat and sprinkle with a tablespoon or so of finely grated Parmesan, or Pecorino. Serve from the pan. The cheese melts and amalgamates with the stock to form a delicious sauce. Eat as a first course, or as an accompaniment to chicken or veal.

A CROWN OF GARLIC TO SURROUND ROAST LAMB

Increasingly I use garlic less as a seasoning, more as a vegetable. I borrowed this idea from the *Observer*'s 'European Cookery' series.

Depending on size, allow anything up to a dozen cloves of garlic per person. Separate and put in a pan of cold water. Bring to the boil and blanch for 2–3 minutes. Drain and refresh. Slice off the root and peel off the skin. If you squeeze the clove gently, more often than not it should pop out of its own accord. As well as making the skinning easier, the preliminary blanching removes any acrid tang and makes the garlic easier to digest.

The garlic can now be cooked in one of two ways. Either melt a little butter or olive oil in a small pan and cook gently until soft and golden, up to 10 minutes. Keep the heat low and watch them in the later stages – once soft they begin to disintegrate which spoils their looks. Alternatively, transfer the garlic to a little ovenware dish, moisten with stock and a lump of butter, cover and cook in the oven with the lamb. I put them in 10 minutes or so before the lamb comes out and leave them in a moderate oven while the lamb is resting. They need 30–40 minutes in all but much depends on their size, so check from time to time that all is well and that they don't dry up. Any stock left over can be reduced, and used to coat the cloves with a sticky glaze. Serve the lamb surrounded by the garlic.

GARLIC PURÉE

Separate the cloves from at least 5 heads of garlic – it is not worth doing less – and put them in a pan of water. Bring to the boil and blanch for 5 minutes. Drain, peel and repeat the blanching process three more times. Finally, cook the garlic in fresh water for another 5–10 minutes by which time they should be soft as butter. Drain thoroughly and purée in a blender until absolutely smooth. Add salt to taste. The purée is now ready and can be kept under a film of olive oil in the refrigerator until required. Transfer to a glass jar, press it down well making sure there are no air holes, as this will cause it to spoil, and cover with oil.

This beautiful purée can be used in several ways. Blend it – sparingly, a teaspoon at a time – with olive oil, spread generously on rounds of dry baked bread and grill until the surface is lightly browned and the croûtes have warmed through. Serve with soups, crudités, or on their own as canapés. Use as a base for a garlic soup or as a garlicky flavouring in other soups. Thin down with good stock, meat juices, creamy milk or single cream and you have an unctuous sauce for serving with poached chicken, with lamb cutlets, with pigeon and, perhaps best of all, with poached eggs nestling in a bed of potato purée, served with some crisply cooked, green cabbage. Ambrosial.

MARROW STUFFED WITH CRAB

I must be one of the few people who do not consider marrow to be fit only for the harvest festival. The trick, of course, is to catch them young. Then they have a delicate, almost buttery flavour, to my mind finer than courgettes.

For 4 marrows, 6 in / 15 cm long
2 oz / 60 g cracked wheat; approx. 6 oz / 170 g fresh crab meat; 2 fat spring onions, softened in a knob of butter; 1–2 teaspoons each of finely chopped dill and parsley; a little vegetable oil.

Try and choose marrows about 6 in / 15 cm long but larger ones will do too. Cut them in half, scoop out the seeds and pre-cook them in a little water for 10–15 minutes. This is important; the final cooking then takes half the time and the stuffing retains its fresh flavour.

Pour boiling water over the cracked wheat and leave to soften for 5 minutes or so. Drain and squeeze out the excess moisture. You should now have about 6 oz / 170 g in weight. You want approximately the same amount of crab meat. Lightly mix all the stuffing ingredients and set aside. When the marrow is cool enough to handle, paint the outsides and edges with vegetable oil and fill the cavities with the stuffing. Transfer to a greased oven dish, cover loosely with foil and cook in a moderate oven for about 30 minutes, or until the marrow is tender. Serve as a first course or as part of a summer vegetable meal, with a fresh tomato *coulis* to accompany. A good dish for courgettes also. I do not recommend using frozen crab meat for this dish. Use fresh, and make soup with the shell and debris. See p. 39.

STUFFED MUSHROOMS IN VINE LEAVES
A vine is almost worth growing for its leaves alone. They have just the right amount of chewiness and a lovely lemony flavour, especially good when filled with stuffings (dolmades must be one of the nicest, cheapest dishes in the world) or wrapped around vegetables, fish and game. This is a summer dish, for eating out of doors, cooked over charcoal, or cold as part of a mixed *mezze*.

4–8 fresh vine leaves; 4 large, open-capped mushrooms; large clove of garlic; 2 large, ripe tomatoes; handful of basil and parsley leaves; olive oil; lemon juice.

Blanch the vine leaves in boiling water for 1–2 minutes, drain and refresh in cold water. Spread them out, smooth side down, and cut away the stalk. Wipe the mushrooms, take out the stalks and place each one, dark side uppermost on a vine leaf (or two overlapping each other if they're on the small side). Skin the tomatoes and chop with the garlic and the herbs to a sauce-like consistency, adding the mushroom stalks if you have no other use for them. Spoon the stuffing over the mushrooms and wrap each mushroom in its vine leaf enclosing the stuffing. Either brush with olive oil and grill over charcoal for 5–10 minutes, taking care that the leaves do not char too much, or bake in a shallow dish with a little water and tablespoon of olive oil in a moderate oven for 30 minutes or so, basting occasionally. Eat hot, or cool dressed with a little olive oil and lemon juice.

ONION FONDUE
A beautifully mellow dish, especially good with beef or lamb. The original inspiration came from Ambrose Heath, though whether he would have approved of this version I cannot say.

1 lb / 450 g onions, finely sliced; 4 oz /120 g fresh tomatoes; 5 fl oz / 150 ml lamb or beef stock; 1 clove; $\frac{1}{2}$ in / 1$\frac{1}{4}$ cm stick of cinnamon; bay leaf; $\frac{1}{3}$–$\frac{1}{2}$ oz / 10–15 g butter.

Melt a good knob of butter in a heavy pan and gently cook the onions until yellow and soft, about 15–20 minutes. Keep the lid on and stir them around from time to time. Meanwhile prepare the tomatoes. Chop them, blend to a purée and pass through a sieve, pressing through as much of the flesh as you can. When the onions are sufficiently soft, add the rest of the ingredients and continue to cook gently with the lid slightly ajar until all is thick and almost jam-like in consistency. This may take an hour or even a little longer. Stir now and then, and half way through the cooking check the taste, removing the cinnamon and clove when you judge the flavour to be right – they should not dominate, but provide a hint of something warm and faintly spicy. Serve in a shallow dish. This reheats beautifully.

JUGGED PEAS

A period piece, from Mrs Leyel's *Gentle Art of Cookery*. Not a recipe one would want to use frequently, but for older peas it's admirable.

Put your shelled peas in a glass jar which has a tight fitting lid – a bottling jar is ideal. Add a couple of knobs of butter, a teaspoon of sugar, a few shredded lettuce leaves and a couple of chopped spring onions. Screw the lid on tightly and place the jar in a saucepan of boiling water which comes half way up the jar. A pressure cooker, minus the weights, is the thing to use if you have one. Cover and cook briskly, allowing 40 minutes for older peas and 25 minutes for younger ones. The peas cook in their own juice. For a grander dish, thicken the juices with an egg yolk mixed with a little single cream and serve the peas surrounded by triangles of toasted bread.

FLUFFY PARSNIPS

An excellent idea, from Natalie Hambro's *Particular Delights*, which turns the meaty parsnip into a light and airy affair. I have made only the slightest amendments.

12 oz / 340 g diced parsnip; 1 egg.
Optional seasonings: 1 teaspoon brown sugar; butter; grated nutmeg; pepper; crisply fried bacon bits.

Remove any woody centres from the parsnips and cook them in a little water in a covered pan until soft. Whizz the egg in a food processor for a few seconds, add the drained parsnips and blend for 1–2 minutes. The purée will fluff up dramatically. If your parsnips were sweet and fine-flavoured the purée will be excellent as it is. Lesser parsnips may need – and you may prefer – additional seasoning of sugar, a lump of butter and pepper. Transfer the purée to a heated serving dish. Embellish, if you wish, with a meagre sprinkling of nutmeg and a scattering of crisply fried bacon pieces. Serve as part of a vegetable meal, or to accompany roast beef or game. A plain celeriac and potato purée (⅓ celeriac, ⅔ potato) is excellent made this way also.

RUMBLEDETHUMPS

A recipe – if that's the right word – from Ambrose Heath's *Vegetable Dishes and Salads*. It makes me smile; it may not be *haute cuisine*, but I doubt if there are many dishes quite like it.

'NORTH: May I ask, with all due solemnity, what *are* rumbledethumps?
SHEPHERD: Something like Mr Hazlitt's character of Shakespeare. Take a peck of purtatoes, and put them into a boyne [large pot] – at them with a beetle – a dab of butter – the beetle again – another dab – then cabbage – purtato – beetle and dab – saut [salt] meanwhile – and a shake o' common black pepper – feenally, cabbage and purtato throughither – pree [taste], and you'll fin' them decent rumbledethumps.' [A beetle is a potato masher.]

SUNSET PURÉE

The north east of England is not generally known for gastronomic excellence but we have our bright spots. One is the Tontine Restaurant at Staddlebridge, run by the McCoy brothers. There I was much intrigued by a vibrant orange-red carrot and red pepper purée, a combination new to me and very delicious. 'Could they possibly. . .' They could and did, willingly and generously. This is the recipe as it was given to me. Take a quantity of red peppers, say 2 lb / 900 g. Sweat in a little olive oil with a scrap of garlic until they're very soft. Purée until smooth and set aside. Take about half the quantity of carrots and boil them in an inch or so of water until they, too, are very soft and the water has all but disappeared. Purée, beat in about a teaspoon of butter and set aside also. Now start adding the carrot purée to the red pepper purée stopping when the taste seems right to you. Season to taste and then add a dash of red wine vinegar and a good pinch of cayenne. These last two seasonings make all the difference.

Make sure both purées are very smooth, adding a little carrot water or plain water if necessary. Quantities can be varied to suit, as can the proportions of pepper to carrot. One of the prettiest of purées.

SCORZONERA WITH MUSTARD AND CHERVIL SAUCE

Scorzonera (and its close relation, the white-skinned salsify) is not common in greengrocers' though large supermarkets like Sainsbury's give it shelf space for those curious enough to be tempted by this delicate, long, black-skinned tuber which digs deep into the soil for minerals that other vegetables miss. It is a good vegetable to serve on its own as a first course.

Allow 2–3 tubers per person and scrub under the tap. Peel off the skin with a potato peeler and rub the milky-white surfaces with a cut lemon. Chop into lengths about the size of your little finger and cook gently in a knob of butter, turning frequently, for 7–10 minutes. Adjust the heat should they brown too much – a hint of colour is all that's required. Now moisten with enough single cream and water, half and half, to cover the base of the pan and form a small amount of sauce. Stir and continue cooking until tender, another 10 minutes or so is usually enough, and replenish the sauce with a little more water if it dries up too much. Finish with a teaspoon or less of mild German mustard and a little finely chopped chervil to taste. Divide between small heated plates and serve immediately.

VEGETABLE STEWS

A great standby, especially in winter, and of infinite variety. Remember that small amounts of vegetables grow into sizeable stews.

As a general guide, include a selection of root vegetables, a pulse such as lentils or butter beans, and some green vegetables to be added at the end. Keep flavourings simple – bay leaves, a fresh chilli to add bite, garlic and onions and, maybe, a few chopped herbs to finish.

Here are two examples of the kind of stews I make. The method is the same for both.

(1) 4 oz / 120 g dried butter beans, soaked and simmered in fresh water until almost cooked; 3–4 sticks celery; 2 large carrots; 2 large potatoes; small white cabbage; 4–6 oz / 120–170 g french beans / peas / courgettes; small onion; 2 leeks; 1–2 cloves garlic, crushed; large bay leaf; finely chopped parsley; milk and water.

(2) 4 oz / 120 g split lentils; large onion; 2 parsnips; stick celery; 2 large potatoes; small cauliflower; 8 oz / 225 g Brussels sprouts; large tin tomatoes, sieved; fresh chilli, seeds removed and chopped; 1 dessertspoon tomato purée; sprig of thyme; water.

Clean the root vegetables, peel and dice as appropriate. Shred cabbage, slice onions and leeks, dice beans and celery, slice courgettes, divide cauliflower into florets.

Sweat the root vegetables and onions in a large pan in a good knob of butter, ghee, or vegetable oil, together with chilli and garlic if used, for 5–10 minutes. Add the pulses, tomatoes, seasonings and water or milk and water barely to cover. Cook until the vegetables are tender, adding the green vegetables towards the end. Check the seasoning and serve. Brown rice or bulgur makes a good accompaniment. The potatoes and pulses act as natural thickeners for these stews but a little potato flour slaked in water can be added if necessary at the end. Wonderful hang-over food.

GREEK-STYLE BEANS
The standard tomato, onion and bean stew, well-known and loved and ideal for any french or bobby bean past its prime. Quantities are a moveable feast according to taste and supply, though this is not a dish worth making for less than 1 lb / 450 g of beans. As it keeps in the fridge for up to a week you might as well make it in bulk when beans and tomatoes are at their cheapest and best. As a rough guide, for every 1 lb / 450 g or so of beans allow 1 large sliced onion, at least half the weight of beans in fresh tomatoes, and a large clove of garlic. You will also need a generous amount of chopped parsley, probably some tomato purée, ½ teaspoon or so of sugar, and olive oil for frying.

Top and tail the beans, cut into 2 in / 5 cm lengths and set aside. Heat enough olive oil to cover the base of a casserole large enough to hold the stew and gently sweat the onion and garlic until soft. Keep the lid on and don't let them catch. Pile the beans on top, then the tomatoes, roughly chopped, and sprinkle chopped parsley over the whole. Add a good pinch of sugar, cover, leaving the lid slightly ajar, and cook over a moderate heat until the beans are tender and the sauce is thick and well-flavoured – anything from 30–45 minutes. After about 15 minutes give everything a stir to distribute the layers, and towards the end of the cooking time check the sauce – our tomatoes cannot compare with those from hot countries so be prepared to compensate with a little tomato purée. You may need to raise the heat at the end should the sauce still be a little watery.

Leave to cool, preferably for 24 hours, before serving at room temperature, as a first course, with pitta bread. One of my favourite summer dishes.

MEXICAN-STYLE BEANS

A spicy variation on the tomato and vegetable stew theme, well suited to runner beans or courgettes as well as french beans. To be eaten hot or cold. It keeps well and, like Greek-style beans, will freeze if necessary.

1 lb / 450 g beans; 2 tablespoons olive oil; 1 large onion, sliced; 1 in / 2.5 cm stick of cinnamon; heaped tablespoon fresh chopped coriander; 1 fresh chilli, seeds removed and chopped; 1 dessertspoon tomato purée; 2 large tomatoes, roughly chopped; clove of garlic, crushed and chopped.

Top and tail the beans. Slice runner beans diagonally, thick or thin as you prefer, and chop french beans into 2 in / 5 cm chunks. Slice courgettes also. Sweat the onion, chilli and garlic until soft and golden, add all the other ingredients, give the stew a stir, cover as before, and cook fairly gently until the tomatoes have produced a nice thick sauce and the vegetables are tender. Remember to stir from time to time. The cinnamon adds a hint of unexpected warmth and the coriander gives the dish a heady fragrance.

SAFFRON CRÊPES WITH VEGETABLE FILLINGS

Crêpes are made from the same ingredients as pancakes but in different proportions. They are altogether thinner, lighter and more delicate fare. Flavoured with saffron and brandy and filled, they take on an elegance which belies their simplicity and their cost. They make as nice a start to a meal as you could wish for.

For approximately 8 pancakes
2 eggs; ½ oz / 15 g plain flour; 1 dessertspoon melted butter or olive oil; healthy pinch of powdered saffron; 2 tablespoons brandy; approx. 3–4 fl oz / 100 ml milk, milk and water or water; pinch of salt (optional).

Sift the flour and salt, if used, into a bowl. Make a well in the centre and break in the eggs. Using either a fork or small whisk, incorporate the flour into the eggs adding the brandy and enough liquid to give the batter the consistency of thin cream. A little experience soon shows how much liquid your batter needs. Stir in the saffron, reduced to powder by setting the strands under a low grill for a few minutes to dry out and then crumbled between the fingers, and continue to mix the batter until no lumps of flour remain. Set aside for a few minutes or use straightaway. Just before using, stir in the melted fat.

Set a small heavy omelette pan over a low heat and, when it has heated through, add a knob of butter or a little oil. Taking care not to burn your fingers, wipe the pan round with a ball of kitchen paper. This will coat it with the thinnest film of fat and saves worry about the crêpes sticking. Ladle in enough batter to cover the base of the pan thinly, tipping the pan round quickly so that it coats evenly. About 1½–2 tablespoons is usually enough; if there's any excess, tip it back into the bowl. The batter should sizzle slightly as it hits the pan. Keeping the heat moderately low, cook the *crêpe* until the underside is brown and the edges have begun to curl, a couple of minutes or so. Flip over, cook for a few more seconds and turn out on to a warm plate. The first is usually the least successful so don't worry if it's slightly less than perfect. Cook all the *crêpes* in the same way, stirring the batter each time as the contents tend to settle. Should the pan seem to be drying out, wipe again with your bit of kitchen paper. I find it's sensible to cook all the pancakes together and keep them warm in a low oven, wrapped in foil. Alternatively they can be prepared in advance, wrapped in cling film and reheated later.

The fillings can be as varied as you wish. I prefer to keep them simple and of the type which can be assembled quickly. In this respect purées such as the one on p. 73 are ideal; prepared in advance, they can then be kept hot over a pan of hot water whilst you're seeing to the *crêpes* and the whole dish assembled in a matter of moments. Lay the *crêpes* on hot plates, spoon the filling down the centre, roll and serve with the folds tucked underneath.

Savoury spinach and stir-fried Chinese vegetable mixtures are two other obvious choices. One of my favourites is broccoli florets blanched for a minute in boiling water, chopped and tossed in a pan with a mixture of lightly fried raisins and pine kernels. Or skinned and chopped, ripe tomatoes tossed in a little tarragon butter for 3–4 minutes, just long enough for the juices to run and form their own savoury sauce. Or grate some courgettes, squeeze out the excess moisture with your hands or in a sieve, and then cook them for 30 seconds (no more) over a high heat in a little butter or oil. Stir in a pat of savoury butter or *pesto*, and fill the crêpes in the usual way.

You can omit the saffron; change the flavour by adding some finely chopped herbs to the batter mix; serve the *crêpes* plain or sauced, or simply dribble a little cream or fresh tomato sauce across the centre. You can make them more substantial by adding savoury cheese or fish mixtures. The possibilities are endless.

MIXED VEGETABLE HORS D'OEUVRE

A variation on the vegetables *à la grecque* theme, adapted from Richard Olney's *Simple French Food*.

For the base: 1 medium onion, sliced; 2–4 cloves of garlic, sliced; 12 oz / 340 g chopped fresh tomatoes / large can of sieved tomatoes / fresh tomato sauce; ½ pint / 300 ml dry white wine; heaped teaspoon coriander seeds; 1 oz / 30 g dried raisins; bay leaf; sprig of thyme; 1 dessertspoon chopped oregano; pinch of cayenne; 1 teaspoon black peppercorns; juice of lemon; 1 teaspoon sugar; 2–4 tablespoons olive oil.

Mixed vegetables – a selection from: courgettes, sugar snap peas, cauliflower, button mushrooms, fennel, artichoke hearts, broad beans, leeks, baby onions, celery, red and green peppers, french beans.

Choose a heavy casserole which will take the vegetables comfortably. Melt enough olive oil to cover the base and gently sweat the onion until soft and limpid but not coloured, about 20 minutes or so. Keep the pan covered during this time and stir the onion around to prevent it from catching. Add the tomatoes and the garlic and continue to cook for another 10 minutes, again stirring often. Have your selection of vegetables previously prepared and cut or sliced into appropriately sized pieces. Add them a few at a time to the pan, stirring them round in the sauce. Add the seasonings, the wine and the lemon juice, stir, bring to the boil over a brisk heat and then simmer gently, covered, for about 30–40 minutes. Remove the vegetables with a slotted spoon and transfer to a serving dish. Boil the sauce vigorously until just enough remains to moisten the vegetables. Distribute the sauce evenly over the vegetables, cool, cover and keep in the refrigerator until required. It will easily keep for 4–5 days. Just before serving, sprinkle with chopped herbs of your choice and serve either chilled or, preferably, at room temperature.

This recipe works well with almost any combination of vegetables. The selection need not be large but try to include both soft and crunchy elements. The base can be reduced or increased according to the amount of vegetables used. As for flavourings, the last word rests with Richard Olney: 'If the raisins seem bizarre to you, leave them out; if you have no taste for coriander, leave it out; the dish will lose its Oriental distinction but will not, otherwise, be the worse for the omissions. If the presence of crunchy, hot peppercorns is distressing, leave them out.'

Potatoes   *What I say is that, if a man really likes potatoes, he must be a pretty decent sort of fellow.*
A. A. MILNE *Not That It Matters*, 1919

POMMES NATURE

There can be no finer way to cook new potatoes than in their own juices with nothing but a lump of butter. They retain all their flavour and take on a slight nuttiness from the browned butter. Choose small, even-sized potatoes, scrub, and scrape or not as you prefer. Melt a generous knob of unsalted butter or, better, clarified butter, just enough to cover the base of a heavy pan which will hold the potatoes snugly in a single layer. Add the potatoes, cover and cook over the lowest heat possible, shaking the pan from time to time. The potatoes will take from about 20–35 minutes depending on their size.

As long as the pan is heavy and the heat low, the potatoes will not burn and will cook in their own juices (potatoes are 75 per cent moisture). Should you be nervous, never having cooked potatoes this way before, by all means add a couple of tablespoons of water. The potatoes will not be the same but still very good.

BLACK KNIGHTS

For buffets, parties, and what is engagingly termed finger food. Scrub and cook tiny, even-sized potatoes, either in a steamer or in a covered pan with a little water or wrapped in foil in the oven until they are soft. Leave to cool until barely warm, then score the skin along the top to a depth of $\frac{1}{4}$ in / $\frac{1}{2}$ cm or so. Squeeze the potatoes gently to open them out a little and fill each one with a teaspoon of thick, sour cream flavoured, if you like, with a little lemon juice. *Crème fraîche* or *quark* are other possibilities. Decorate each potato with a little caviar or smoked salmon and place in a black paper case. No other colour will do. If you cannot buy them, raid a chocolate box. Arrange the potatoes on a plain white serving plate and serve as soon as possible.

RED MOJO SAUCE

A dipping sauce from the Canary Islands, often served as *tapas*, for tiny hot new potatoes, cooked in their skins in the oven until soft and wrinkled. Despite its name the sauce is a muddy brown but fiery and spirited nonetheless. The sensation of hot potato with chilled mojo sauce is explosive.

2–3 cloves of garlic; 1 teaspoon cumin seeds; 1 teaspoon paprika; 1 dessertspoon chopped thyme; 4–5 fl oz / 120–150 ml robust olive oil; 1–2 teaspoons wine vinegar or lemon juice; 3–4 tablespoons hot water; salt.

Lightly toast the cumin seeds and pound in a mortar. Add the garlic, crushed and finely chopped and a pinch of salt and pound again to a smooth pulp. Add the paprika and thyme and repeat the process once more. You should now have a homogenous paste. Stir in the olive oil gradually. Sharpen the sauce with a little lemon juice or vinegar and then start adding the hot water, stirring well. The water gives the mixture more of a sauce-like consistency and dilutes its strength. Add until the sauce feels right to you and chill until required. [Serves 3–4.]

SORREL, EGG AND POTATO SALAD
Everyone has their favourite potato salad; this is mine.

4 or 5 hard-boiled eggs; 1 lb / 450 g freshly cooked waxy potatoes; small handful of sorrel leaves; lettuce leaves, preferably of the cabbage type; 3–4 tablespoons mayonnaise; hot water.

First prepare the dressing. Remove the mid-ribs from the sorrel, reserve a couple of the leaves and chop the rest to a purée. Stir into the mayonnaise and dilute to a pouring consistency with a little hot water. Set aside.

   Spread the lettuce leaves on a large platter. Dice the potatoes. Mash one of the eggs till it is finely crumbled and slice the rest. Fill the centre of the salad with the hot, diced potato and spoon over the sorrel mayonnaise. Arrange the egg slices in a border around the potatoes and scatter the crumbled egg over the top of the mayonnaise. Shred the remaining sorrel leaves into fine ribbons and arrange in a single line down the centre. Eat whilst the potatoes are still warm.

LAZY BAKED POTATOES
Cut jacket potatoes in half lengthwise, paint the cut surfaces lightly with oil, and cook them in a very hot oven. They will be ready in about half the usual time. The cut side puffs up attractively, browned and crisp. A nice accompaniment to almost any stew, grilled meat or vegetable dishes.

GARLIC POTATOES

When I cooked these in the *Guardian*/Mouton Cadet cookery competition one of the judges described them as 'odd but wonderful'. See what you think.

For each person allow 1 medium-sized or half a large potato, and 6–8 cloves of garlic. Scrub the potatoes, prick the skins, and bake in the oven until very soft. Meanwhile blanch the cloves of garlic in boiling water for a couple of minutes. Drain and peel off their skins. Reserve half and simmer the remainder in approximately ½ pint / 300 ml of milk until they're absolutely tender – the aroma is exquisite. Blend to a smooth purée and reserve. When the potatoes are done, cut them in half, scoop out the flesh and mash with the warm garlic purée until smooth and creamy, adding a little more milk if necessary. Taste and season lightly with a pinch of salt if needed. Pipe the mixture into half the potato skins, brush with a little melted butter and return to the oven to brown. Serve surrounding a little dish filled with the remaining garlic cloves, lightly fried in a knob of butter and a little olive oil until soft and golden. These you eat with the baked potatoes. 'Odd but wonderful.'

POTATOES SIMMERED IN MILK

Cooking vegetables in milk is a practice long advocated by vegetarians. The milk acts in much the same way as does oil, forming a seal which helps to prevent the dissolution of soluble nutrients into the cooking liquid. I first came across potatoes done this way in one of my most treasured books, Lawrence Hill's *Grow Your Own Fruit and Vegetables*. Later, I found a similar recipe in Elizabeth David. The method was exactly the same but the detail – a judicious sprinkling of herbs and a final browning in the oven – transformed something fairly ordinary into something special.

For every 1 lb / 450 g potatoes, allow about 1 pint / 600 ml of milk. Old ones should be peeled and cut into thick slices, new ones scraped and halved or left whole. Put them in a pan, pour over the cold milk, bring to the boil and simmer very gently, covered, until the potatoes are just cooked. Stir from time to time to prevent them sticking and take care not to allow the milk to rise above a simmer. Transfer the potatoes to an oven-proof dish, arranging them in a single layer. Sprinkle very lightly with nutmeg and some finely chopped basil or thyme. These are the two recommended by Mrs David, but tarragon and oregano also work well, so choose your herbs to match your other dishes. Moisten with 3 or 4 tablespoons of the cooking liquor, saving the rest for soup, and leave uncovered in a moderate oven for 15–20 minutes. The potatoes acquire a lovely golden glow and have a fine, creamy flavour. A potato dish worth eating on its own with a crisp green salad.

POTATOES, PARSNIPS AND CABBAGE
An Irish Country Dish, 1750
1. Boil potatoes and parsnips till they are soft.
2. Mash them with new milk.
3. Add a cabbage boiled tender and cut very small.
4. Mix the whole over the fire with a slice of good butter, some pepper and salt, and eat it hot.

NB – This is recorded by Farmer Ellis, of Little Gaddesdon, Hertfordshire, and resembles the Irish dish 'Champ' and the Devonshire Stew, the recipe of which is dated 1837. All four are closely allied to the stoved 'taties of Aberdeenshire and Dr Kitchiner's 'bubble and squeak'.

FLORENCE WHITE *Good Things in England, 1932*

FANNED POTATOES
These have what Miles Kington once described as the greatest quality of all; 'crispness without, meltingness within'. They also look good, elegant but not over fussy. Choose medium-sized potatoes, preferably a waxy sort like Desirée. Peel them and trim to a neat oval shape. Slice through at $\frac{1}{8}$ in / 0.3 cm intervals, almost but not quite to the bottom of each potato. Dry thoroughly in kitchen paper, gently squeezing them with your hands and pressing them out into a fan shape. Heat a good knob of butter with 2–3 tablespoons of olive oil in a fire-proof dish and turn each potato over in the oil, making sure both sides are coated. This is quicker than painting them with fat, and I generally use my hands. Cook in a fairly hot oven 200°C / 400°F / gas mark 6 or a little higher for about 45 minutes. They are done when the edges are nicely crisped and the insides are soft. Turn them over half way through. Serve surrounding the meat or on a separate platter, arranging them to show off their shape.

REG'S OREGANO POTATOES
One Christmas my brother-in-law, who can never keep out of the kitchen for long, announced that he would cook the potatoes. 'Fine', I said, and watched in astonishment as he proceeded to pour over them a mixture of olive oil, lemon juice and a dried Italian herb mixture he'd

bought me as a present. They were then roasted in the usual way and were excellent.

Roast potatoes do not soak up as much fat as one imagines. Whereas chips are dreadful, with a threefold increase in calorific value, roast potatoes, depending on their size, only increase it by about half. The moral is obvious: keep them larger, rather than smaller.

1½ lb / 675 g even-sized potatoes, peeled and halved lengthwise; 3–4 tablespoons fruity olive oil; 4 tablespoons strained lemon juice; 1 tablespoon chopped oregano or 1–2 teaspoons dried Italian herbs.

Arrange the potatoes in a single layer in a roasting tin which will just hold them comfortably. Pour over the lemon, oil and herb mixture, and roast in the usual way, basting from time to time. They should emerge golden brown, crusty and speckled with herbs. Excellent with roast poultry, veal chops, or grilled or roast lamb.

POTATO AND CELERY JULIENNE

This is a recipe I have been using for many years. It's a natural choice for game or for baked ham but is a useful dish with other vegetables or with grains and pulses.

1 shallot or ½ small onion, finely chopped; 3–4 medium waxy potatoes; 6–8 stalks of celery; knob of butter for frying; finely chopped parsley.

Exact quantities are difficult to give and are best judged by the eye. Aim to have two roughly equal piles of vegetables. Pare off the stringy bits from the celery using a potato peeler and cut into thin *julienne* strips about 2 in / 5 cm long. Peel the potatoes, cutting them slightly thicker – the size of thin chips is about right – keeping the two vegetables separate. Melt a good knob of butter in a large and heavy frying pan, add the celery and the onion and shake over the heat for 4–5 minutes. Add the potatoes, cover, and cook gently for 20–25 minutes until the potatoes are tender. Give them an occasional stir from time to time to prevent them from sticking to the pan over much. Sprinkle with parsley and serve from the pan.

LEMON CRUSTED POTATOES

Cook your potatoes in their skins until they're just cooked. When they're cool enough to handle, using a cloth or kitchen paper to protect your hands, skin, cube, and set aside. Finely chop a small onion and sweat in a knob of butter in an ovenproof dish until soft. Add the finely grated rind and juice of a lemon and a couple of tablespoons of chopped dill or parsley. Add the potatoes to the dish, toss in the savoury mixture and bake in a hot oven for about 15–20 minutes until the potatoes are nicely golden. Taste, add extra lemon juice if necessary, and serve from the same pan. Good with grilled fish, chicken or lamb.

Use firm potatoes for this dish. You will find that the herbs affect the flavour more than you would imagine. In this respect it's a very adaptable dish – chervil, tarragon or fresh coriander can all be used with success.

HOT POT POTATOES
A good winter dish.

generous 1–1¼ lb / 450–570 g waxy potatoes, peeled and finely sliced; 1 extra large onion; approx. ¾ pt / 450 ml lamb or beef stock; 1 tablespoon olive oil plus knob of butter; 2 tablespoons Parmesan cheese.

Peel and slice the onion fairly finely, and sweat over a low heat in the oil and butter in a covered pan until soft and limp. Give it a good 20–25 minutes and stir from time to time. Butter a large shallow ovenproof dish and lay the potatoes in overlapping slices in a single neat layer. Distribute the onion mixture evenly over the top, and pour in enough hot stock to cover the base of the dish almost to the level of the potatoes. Cover with foil and bake for about 1½ hours in a moderately hot oven, 180–190°C / 350–375°F / gas mark 4–5, or until the potatoes are done when tested with a skewer. Remove the foil for the last half hour or so to brown the surface and to allow the edges of the potatoes and onions to crisp up. Check the liquid level also. During the cooking it will reduce to form a slightly thickened sauce. If it looks like drying up too much add a little more liquid. Towards the end, sprinkle over the Parmesan cheese. Return to the oven for a final 7–10 minutes until the cheese, too, has melted and crisped slightly. Serve from the same dish.

POTATOES, FRENCH BEANS, AND WALNUT OIL
Arrange some hot cooked potatoes, cut into chunks, in the bottom of large soup plates or shallow dishes. Add a layer of freshly blanched french beans cut into 1½ in / 4 cm sections on top, and dribble a little walnut oil over them both. Finish with a thick scattering of chopped parsley. A few tiny cubes of either Gruyère cheese or frizzled continental

sausage can be added with the beans. Eat hot, from the same dish, with a plain green salad and grilled, skinned red peppers marinated in olive oil. The kind of food I like best of all.

POTATO CRÊPES

Potato pancakes in various guises are to be found in every country which has taken the potato to heart. This one is French and one of the simplest and best. When I want a quick and savoury potato meal for myself this, or the dish that follows, is the one I usually opt for.

For four people [as an accompanying vegetable] you need about 1–1¼ lb / 450–570 g potatoes, a large beaten egg, 2–3 tablespoons olive oil and, if you wish, some seasonings. Scrape or peel the potatoes, grate on a coarse grater and mix with the beaten egg. The mixture can now be seasoned – a little nutmeg, paprika, finely chopped herbs, garlic, or a spoonful of *pesto* can all be used to good effect but, equally, are all optional. The simplicity of the plain *crêpe* should not be forsaken lightly; the others, though good, serve more to ring the changes. Add salt and pepper to taste, if you wish.

Traditionally the *crêpe* is cooked in one large frying pan but, as it has to be turned over half way through, two smaller ones make for easier handling. Make sure the pan has a good thick bottom and is the kind which will not stick.

Heat enough olive oil to cover the base of the pan(s), tipping it round to get an even coating. When hot, add the potato mixture. It should sizzle slightly when it hits the pan. Press the mixture down with a fish slice, smoothing out the surface and let it sit over a gentle heat for 10–15 minutes. It should cook evenly and gently. If you're using a small pan(s) the *crêpes* should turn without any difficulty. Loosen the sides and underneath with a palette knife, lift it out, smear the pan with a little more olive oil and carefully turn it over. Press down the uncooked side and continue cooking for another 10 minutes or so. With a large pan, loosen as before and then cover the pan with a plate. Using oven gloves, tip the pan upwards and over slightly so that the *crêpe* transfers to the plate. Return the uncooked side to the pan and proceed as before. Alternatively, slide the *crêpe* on to a plate, cover with a second plate, invert the whole thing so that the uncooked side is now uppermost and carry on as usual. When cooked, both sides should be nicely crisped and lightly browned and the centre slightly soft. Serve immediately cut into wedges. A green salad and a fresh tomato sauce go well with this.

POTATO PIZZA

A recipe which grew out of the last. A quickly made meal-in-one for one or two people.

Potato crêpe mixture as above; sliced tomatoes; Feta or Mozzarella cheese; stoned, chopped, black olives; finely chopped oregano and mint.

Make the potato crêpe(s) as before in a small pan(s) up to the stage when it's been turned over and the other side is about to be cooked. Think of the surface as a pizza and arrange slices of tomato and the thinly sliced cheese neatly over the top. Add a few stoned black olives, a liberal scattering of herbs, cover and cook for the remaining 10 minutes. Ease out gently and serve. Vary fillings to suit, but keep them piquant and well-balanced.

For one, allow 8 oz / 225 g grated potato and half an egg.

Meat

If it were done, when tis done,
then t'were well it were done quickly.

Inscription over the gridiron of the Sublime Sociey of Beefsteaks,
1735–1866

There has been a noticeable shift of emphasis in our attitudes to meat.
Increasing concern over animal fats, modern rearing techniques and
production line butchering have led many of us to question the real
value of meat and its role in our diet. As a result we are beginning to eat
less meat and to eat it less often.

This change of heart has brought real benefits. With meat no longer
the star attraction, our diet has become more varied. The possibility of
using it as a flavouring rather than the main ingredient in a dish has
opened up new horizons. Stir-fry now jostles happily with cottage pie.
We are also learning to pay for quality and to treat our meat with new
respect. Gone are the complicated, extravagant dishes and the
nondescript casseroles. In their place, simpler things – a loin of lamb
plainly roasted, the occasional heady daube, a light, summery sauté or a
sticky oxtail stew. Game cookery, our particular forte, is coming into its
own. Unsullied so far by unsavoury farming practices, and lower in fat,
it makes fine eating and good sense.

ROAST SIRLOIN OF BEEF

The roasting joint *par excellence*, expensive, but with careful management, excellent value. It is not worth buying less than about 5½ lb /2½ kg total weight. This will provide ample hot and cold roast beef, a strip of flank and anything from 1 lb / 450 g upwards of beef fillet. I never roast either of these with the joint. The flank, depending on its size, goes for minced beef or is braised in a piece with onions, wine and tomatoes. Served with pasta it makes an excellent mid-week dish. The fillet is saved for *boeuf en croûte*, steaks, Stroganoff or *Carpaccio*. The bones go for stock and any odd bits go for Chinese, cottage pie or rissoles. This way it is possible to get three to four and sometimes more first class meals out of your beef.

Preheat the oven to 240°C / 475°F / gas mark 9 and weigh the joint. Set in a roasting tin fat side uppermost, i.e. along the length of the rib bone, on a trivet if you wish. Seal the joint at this high temperature for 10 minutes. Turn the oven down to 220°C / 425°F / gas mark 7 and continue cooking until the joint begins to shrink and smells like beef, basting a couple of times during the cooking.

As a general guideline calculate the cooking time at 15 minutes to the pound. This should give you a couple of outside slices of medium-done beef with the rest beautifully graded from done, on the outside, to rare next to the bone, with everything in between very pink. I find that a 3 ribbed joint, weighing about 3¾ lb / 1¾ kg takes 45–50 minutes for rare beef. If you prefer beef less red, you will need to add 15–30 minutes extra cooking time, depending on the size of the joint. Transfer the beef to a warm dish, cover loosely with foil, and leave in a warm place to settle.

I find it easier to take the meat off the bone before carving it into fine, thin slices. I serve the Yorkshire pudding first, straight from the oven, sizzling hot, with gravy. The beef is served separately with a few potatoes. Other vegetables come before or after the beef. The bone is the cook's perk.

Roasting a joint of meat may be simple but it is by no means easy. A small joint will cook more quickly than a large one which, in turn, will hold its temperature and continue cooking out of the oven longer. Few of us are likely to be roasting prime sirloin or other joints of meat very often, so it is sensible to keep a record – weight, cooking time and temperature, what it looked like and how it tasted, jotted down in a small notebook.

Red meat must be well hung. Most of the tenderising process for beef continues up to ten days after slaughter so there seems little point in buying any which has not been hung for at least this time. This is where a good butcher is worth his weight in gold. The meat will cost more – meat can lose up to 2 per cent of its weight when hung properly – but it will always be worth it. Lamb too benefits from a week's hanging. If I want lamb for a weekend, I buy it early in the week and keep it in an unheated room in winter or in the refrigerator at other times of the year. I order beef at least two weeks in advance.

After cooking a brief resting period is essential. This allows the fibres which have contracted during cooking to relax. Cover the meat loosely with foil and leave in a warm place. Large joints will keep their heat for up to an hour, so there is never any problem of the meat getting cold. Even small pieces of meat, lamb cutlets for example, improve by being kept warm for five minutes or so.

BOEUF MIROTON
The classic French way of using up left-over roast beef and one of the best winter meat dishes.

Finely slice $1-1\frac{1}{2}$ lb / 450–675 g of large onions and sweat them very gently in a good knob of butter or beef dripping with a bay leaf in a covered pan until soft and golden, at least 15 minutes and longer if you can. Add a tablespoon of flour and enough beef stock to make a thick sauce. Continue cooking for another 15–20 minutes, adding a little more stock if necessary. Stir in a teaspoon or more, to taste, of Dijon mustard and transfer the sauce to a shallow ovenproof dish. Lay thin slices of cold roast beef, slightly overlapping, on top. Cover and cook on top of the stove just enough to warm the beef through and no more as the beef inclines to toughen. Sprinkle with a little finely chopped parsley and serve from the same pan accompanied by plainly cooked or jacket potatoes.

CARPACCIO OF BEEF
The Italian version of *steak tartare*. The formula is the same, raw beef with savoury additions, but the method is different. Here slices of fillet of beef are beaten out to paper thinness and served with a highly piquant sauce. It is an excellent way of making a small quantity of fillet go a very long way. Treat it like smoked salmon and serve in small quantities as a first course of a grander than usual meal. The taste is surprisingly delicate and un-beef like.

8–10 oz / 225–280 g prime fillet of beef, trimmed of any fat and silvery skin and well chilled.

For the sauce: 6 anchovy fillets; small piece of garlic (optional); 1 heaped tablespoon each of finely chopped shallot, capers and gherkins; 1 tablespoon Dijon mustard; 2–3 teaspoons wine vinegar; 3–4 fl oz / 90–120 ml olive, groundnut or safflower oil.

First make the sauce. The exact flavourings are a matter of personal taste. If onions, for example, are disagreeable to you leave them out. It should however be sharp, piquant with no one taste dominating. Put everything into a blender or food processor and blend to a smooth cream. It is best to build up the sauce slowly, adding the ingredients gradually and tasting after each addition until the flavour seems right.

The beef must be free of any skin, connective tissue or fat. Slice it thinly with a razor sharp knife. Taking each slice in turn, beat out with a wooden meat hammer between two sheets of cling film. They will spread considerably. Using a palette knife, carefully peel the beef off and transfer to individual serving plates. Dribble over a little of the sauce from a teaspoon, first in parallel lines and then crossways, to create a lattice effect. Serve the rest of the sauce separately and accompany with thin slices of dark rye bread and a radish salad.

The sauce can be prepared well in advance and will keep in the refrigerator for some time. The beef soon loses its bright, rosy redness and is best prepared just before serving. To keep it longer, cover with cling film and chill in the refrigerator.

OXTAIL IN THE BURGUNDY STYLE

This is a splendid dish, sticky and succulent, one for cold days and worth lavishing care on. You will need to start one or two days in advance of the meal. An oxtail – or at least the ones I buy – inconveniently feeds about three, and my butcher not unreasonably insists on sharing out both the thick, juicy pieces with the boney bits at the end ('Who else will buy them?' he demands). So I buy two and save the very small pieces for soup or stock.

Approx. 3¼ lb / 1½ kg oxtail, cut into 2 in / 5 cm chunks.

For the marinade: 8 fl oz / 225 ml reasonable red wine; 1 onion, sliced; 1 tablespoon olive oil; sprig of thyme, parsley and oregano.

For the cooking: up to 1½ pints / 900 ml beef stock; 1 tablespoon flour;

clove of garlic, crushed; strip of dried orange peel; piece of celery 3 in / 7.5 cm long; medium carrot cut in half; whole tomato; bay leaf; olive oil or beef dripping for frying.

To finish: 16–20 small pickling onions or shallots; 4–6 oz /120–170 g carrots, cut into thin strips; 1 teaspoon sugar; $\frac{1}{3}$–$\frac{1}{2}$ oz / 10–15 g butter.

Put the oxtail and all the marinade ingredients into a large bowl, cover and leave for 4–6 hours at room temperature or overnight in the refrigerator, turning the pieces over half way through. Remove the oxtail, dry on kitchen paper and set aside. Strain the marinade, discarding the onion but keeping back the herbs. Choose a casserole dish into which you can snugly fit the oxtail. Brown a few pieces at a time in a little oil, removing them to a plate as they are done. Once browned, pack them neatly into the casserole, sprinkle over the flour, pour over the marinade and enough stock to cover. Add all the seasonings including the reserved herbs and gently bring to the boil, skimming if necessary. Cover, transfer to a very low oven 130°C / 265°F / gas mark $\frac{1}{2}$ and cook for 3–4 hours or until the meat is just beginning to part from the bone. Be prepared for a little latitude one way or the other. Remove from the oven, cool, and leave in the refrigerator overnight.

Next day remove the abundant layer of fat sitting on the surface. The stock underneath will have set to a jelly. Heat the stew sufficiently to loosen the meat, take out and transfer to a wide, shallow ovenproof dish. Strain the stock into a clean pan and set over a gentle heat. Keeping it at no more than a bare simmer, reduce until you are left with just enough to cover the dish by a depth of $\frac{1}{2}$ in / $1\frac{1}{4}$ cm or so. As it reduces, repeatedly remove the skin that forms. This will help give the dish a fine glossy finish. Pour the reduced stock over the oxtail and cook for another 50–60 minutes, uncovered, in a moderate oven, 180°C / 350°F / gas mark 4. Baste the meat frequently. The meat surfaces darken and take on a glorious, shiny, caramelised appearance and the sauce becomes a rich, dark brown.

Half way through the final cooking prepare the vegetable garnish. Blanch the onions for 2 minutes in boiling water and drain. Should you grow spring onions, those left to grow large are ideal. Cook them gently with the carrots and the butter and sugar in a heavy pan for about 20–25 minutes until nicely caramelised, turning from time to time.

Transfer the meat to a heated serving dish, pour the sauce around and surround with the vegetables. Serve with a creamy potato purée and a plain, undressed salad. Have an empty plate for the bones and a finger bowl at the ready; picking up the bones and sucking out the meat is too great a pleasure to miss.

BRAISED BREAST OF VEAL

Braising is an amiable process, one which takes care of itself and results in beautifully tender and succulent dishes. The meat is cooked gently, in a very slow or slow oven, anything from 80–140°C / 175–285°F / gas mark ¼–1, the length of time depending on the type of meat and the kind of pot you use. Breast of veal is a good choice for a braise. It is meaty, economical and sweet flavoured and yields a fine sauce.

2¼–2¾ lb / 1–1¼ kg breast of veal.

For the stuffing: 4 oz / 120 g mushrooms; small onion; slice of lean boiled ham or tongue; 1 dessertspoon parsley plus 2 sage leaves, both finely chopped; knob of butter.

For the braise: 5 fl oz / 150 ml each of white wine and chicken or veal stock; 2 tablespoons brandy; 2 tablespoons olive oil; piece of carrot and celery; bay leaf; large sprig of tarragon; 1 teaspoon potato flour slaked in water.

Begin with the stuffing. Chop the onions and mushrooms very finely and cook over a fairly brisk heat in a knob of butter till most of the moisture has evaporated. Off the heat, stir in the ham or tongue chopped almost to a paste (a matter of seconds in a food processor), along with the herbs, and allow to cool. The stuffing should be fairly stiff. If it is in any way loose, firm it up with a few soft breadcrumbs. Once cool, spread over the veal, keeping it well away from the edge. Roll the meat into a neat shape and tie with string.

Choose a heavy casserole dish with a tight fitting lid which will just hold the joint comfortably. Brown the veal in the olive oil. Pour on the brandy and, when all but evaporated, add the wine. Let this bubble up and reduce for a couple of minutes before adding the stock. Tuck the rest of the seasonings around the veal, bring gently to the boil, cover and transfer to a very low oven 130°C / 265°F / gas mark ½. Allow 2½–3 hours cooking time, at the end of which the veal should be very tender. Check half way through that all is well and that the liquid no more than shivers. Remove the veal and keep it uncovered in the low oven while you finish the sauce. Strain the stock and soak up the fat with kitchen paper. Return to the pan and boil down if necessary to concentrate the flavour. Thicken slightly with a little potato flour slaked in water – add it gradually, enough to give body but no more. Bring gently back to the boil and set aside. Remove the string from the veal and carve into thick, generous slices. Arrange on a heated serving dish, spoon over the sauce, decorate with a few leaves of tarragon and serve accompanied by rice or pasta and spinach. If you have a quantity of sauce, serve this separately rather than swamp the meat.

This quantity will easily feed 4–6. If more convenient, the veal can be left in its cooking liquor overnight and reheated the next day. Any left over makes excellent cold eating, so much so it's worth cooking extra to allow for this. Carve into thin slices and serve with salads and potatoes.

Ambrose Heath's Veal Kidney Liégeoise
A recipe from Ambrose Heath's last book *A Menu For All Seasons*, published posthumously in 1972. I particularly like his comment on seakale.

'Get a nice veal kidney (one is enough for two), trimming it so that a little of the fat surrounding it remains still adhering, and cook it in a small casserole with butter, basting it well and being careful not to overcook it or it will get leathery. The inside should be a delicate pink when it is cut open and eaten. When it is done, pour into the casserole a liqueur glassful of warmed gin and set it alight. If you can manage to get them, sprinkle the kidney on serving with a little crushed dried juniper berries. If you could find some seakale to eat with this, you would be doing yourself proud.'

The recommended wine was Portuguese Vila Real branco. Smoked sprats to start with, and a chestnut fool to finish.

The recipe adapts well to lamb's kidneys, and can be cooked on top of the stove in a frying pan. Cook briefly with a little crushed juniper berries until just pink and flame with gin.

OSSO BUCO
My favourite veal dish, always better at home than in restaurants where it can be an excuse sometimes for an indifferent tomato and onion and shin of beef stew.

4 large, thick slices of shin of veal, to include the central marrow bone, about 1–2 in / 2.5–5 cm in thickness; 5 fl oz / 150 ml each of Italian white wine and chicken or veal stock; 1–1½ lb / 450–675 g of juicy, ripe tomatoes, coarsely chopped; 1 carrot, stick of celery and small sprig of basil, if available; 2 tablespoons olive oil plus knob of butter for frying.

For the gremolata: small bunch of parsley; clove of garlic; 2 or 3 strips of lemon peel.

Choose a wide, shallow pan and gently brown the pieces of veal on both sides in the oil and butter. Arrange the slices side by side and upright so as not to lose any of the precious marrow. Pour in the wine and let it bubble and reduce for a few minutes. Add the rest of the ingredients. These should come to the top but not completely cover the meat, so adjust the quantity of tomatoes accordingly. Bring to the boil on top of the stove, cover loosely with foil and cook in a low oven 140°C / 285°F / gas mark 1 until the veal is very tender and falling away from the bones. This can take anything from 1½–2½ hours, or even a little longer. I usually err on the long rather than the short side; like all slowly cooked dishes, osso buco is a well-tempered affair.

While the veal is cooking prepare the *gremolata*, as essential to the dish as the marrow in the marrow bone. Chop the parsley, lemon peel and garlic very finely, reducing it to a mass of green, white and yellow speckles, with green predominating. Transfer to a small bowl and set aside until needed.

Transfer the veal to a shallow serving dish and keep warm, uncovered, in the oven. Fish out the seasonings from the sauce and sieve, pressing hard to extract all the juice from the tomato. Return to the pan and boil down to reduce if necessary. The sauce should be thick but not too copious. Check and correct the seasoning, perhaps adding a pinch of sugar or a few drops of basil vinegar. Add any extras cautiously. Pour the sauce around the meat, sprinkle each portion with a little *gremolata* and serve the rest separately. Accompany with plain rice or pasta.

Osso buco can be cooked in advance, so avoiding any anxiety over the timing. Leave in its juices, reheat gently and finish in the usual way.

BRAISED LEG OF LAMB IN THE GREEK STYLE

3¼ lb / 1½ kg leg of lamb, preferably from the fillet end; 12–16 oz / 340–450 g fresh tomatoes, chopped; fresh oregano or dried *rigani*; lemon thyme or thyme; large glass white wine; 4 small, whole bulbs of garlic; olive oil.

Rub the meat with olive oil and seal over a high heat in a heavy frying pan, or on a grillomat, until all the surfaces are well browned. Roll in the chopped herbs and put in a deep casserole dish with a tight fitting lid. Stuff the garlic into the bottom and distribute the chopped tomatoes around the meat. Pour in the wine, bring to the boil, cover, and transfer to a medium hot oven 190°C / 375°F / gas mark 5. Cook for an hour for mainly pink lamb, or for 10–15 minutes longer for medium to well-cooked lamb. Remove from the casserole and leave, loosely covered, in a warm place, for the meat to relax for at least 15 minutes. Longer will not harm. Boil the cooking juices down to form a sauce. Arrange the garlic around the lamb, and serve the sauce separately. Serve with pasta or potatoes and a green salad.

A lovely dish for summer when fresh garlic and summer herbs are about. To eat the garlic, squeeze the pulp from the skins and eat with the lamb.

BEST END OF NECK OF LAMB WITH GRAPEFRUIT AND JUNIPER JELLY

Fruit is always welcome with lamb. This is one of the simpler combinations, for winter when grapefruits are at their best. Juniper jelly goes well with pork and game as well as with lamb. It is a delicate, pale amber, with that faint hint of wildness that characterises all our ancient fruits and berries.

2 pieces of best end of lamb; few sprigs of thyme; large glass of red wine; 1 large, juicy grapefruit, skin and pith removed, divided into segments and all the juice saved; bunch of watercress.

For the juniper jelly: 1 lb / 450 g cooking apples; 1 oz / 30 g pulverised juniper berries; 10 fl oz / 300 ml water; sugar (see method).

Make the juniper jelly in advance. Slice the cooking apples and simmer with the juniper berries and water in a covered pan until the apples are reduced to a pulp, about 40 minutes. Drain overnight in a jelly bag or a sieve lined with a double layer of muslin. This should yield about 10 fl oz / 300 ml of juice. Weigh out an equal amount of sugar, add the juice, stir until the sugar has dissolved and then boil in the usual way until setting point is reached. This should take no more than a couple of minutes. Pot into small, sterilised jars, seal and store.

Get your butcher to chine the joint carefully. If he will also trim the rib bones so much the better though this is easy enough to do at home. Cut away the top 1½ in / 3¾ cm or so of fat and scrape the bones absolutely clean. Score the skin in diamond fashion and preheat the oven to 220°C / 425°F / gas mark 7. Lay the joints, skin side uppermost, in a roasting tin and surround with a few sprigs of thyme. Roast for about 30 minutes for nicely pink lamb and 35 minutes for medium. Remove the meat from the oven and lightly anoint the skin with juniper jelly. Flash under a hot grill for 3–4 minutes to crisp and brown the skin and then let the meat rest, lightly covered in a warm place while you finish the dish.

Discard the thyme and pour off the fat. Have all the other vegetables ready, as finishing the dish needs your undivided attention. Deglaze the pan juices with the wine. Add the juice saved from the grapefruit and boil right down to a sticky glaze. Add the grapefruit segments and turn them lightly so that they warm through and are coated with the glaze. Work quickly and don't leave them for much more than a minute as they can rapidly disintegrate. Arrange on either side of the meat, garnish with watercress and serve with fanned potatoes (see p. 82) and juniper jelly. Winter broccoli, spinach or carrots all make suitable accompaniments.

EPIGRAMMES ITALIENNES
Cheap, delicious, but only worth contemplating if you have the time and enjoy a messy job occasionally.

1 large breast of lamb; 1 sliced onion, leek, carrot and stick of celery; lamb or beef stock; glass of white wine (optional); butter or mutton fat.

To finish: beaten egg; fine dried breadcrumbs; 1 tablespoon Parmesan; 1 pint / 600 ml fresh tomato sauce or tomato vinaigrette.

Start in the morning for that evening's meal or, if more suitable, the day before. Sweat the vegetables in a good knob of butter or mutton fat for about 5 minutes in a pressure cooker pan. Pour over the wine, if you have some handy, and enough stock to cover the base to a depth of $\frac{1}{2}$ in / $1\frac{1}{4}$ cm. Lay the breast of lamb folded over on top. Clamp on the top, bring to high pressure and cook for 35 minutes. Reduce the pressure, take off the lid and leave the meat until it's cool enough to handle. Strain the stock and take off the fat: the broth makes delicious soup. If you don't possess a pressure cooker, braise the lamb in a cool oven for about $2\frac{1}{2}$ hours until very tender. Again leave until cool enough to handle.

Now for the messy bit. Remove the bones and scrape away most of the fat from the outside and between the meat. This is not the conventional way of dealing with *épigrammes* but it is better for your health and digestion, less greasy and more flavoursome. Once the meat has been stripped of most of its fat it will look decidedly ragged but cut it into as neat strips or squares as you can manage, sticking any odd scraps into a respectable shape by pressing them firmly between your hands. Dip first into beaten egg and then into the breadcrumb and Parmesan mixture. Use a palette knife rather than your fingers for this job. Spread the *épigrammes* out on a rack and leave the coating to dry. At this stage they can be left until the next day, in the refrigerator.

For the final cooking, lay the meat in a roasting tin and cook in a hot oven for about 40 minutes until nicely browned and crisp. You will find there is still sufficient fat in them to keep the coating lubricated. Pile into a dish, garnish with watercress and lemon quarters and serve with tomato sauce and jacket potatoes as a main course, or with tomato vinaigrette and salad as a first course.

GREEK PATTIES
A good way of using scraps of lamb left over from a joint.

Mix together a savoury mixture of minced cooked lamb, crumbled Feta or, failing that, cottage cheese, and season with chopped mint, dill or coriander, or with spices such as cinnamon or allspice. A little chopped spring onion or tomato can also be included. Lay a strip of fila pastry about 3 in / 7.5 cm wide on a board, damp all the edges and place a little heap of the mixture about ½ in / 1¼ cm from the edge. Draw the pastry over to enclose the stuffing and form a triangle by bringing the bottom over to the side. Pinch the edges together. Continue folding this way along the length of the strip, ending up with a triangular shaped samosa-like patty three or four layers thick. Make the rest in the same way and arrange on a baking sheet. Brush each side with a little melted butter or olive oil and cook in a hot oven for about 20 minutes until the pastry is crisp and beginning to brown. Serve as a first course with a yoghurt dressing, cold tomato and mint sauce or tomato vinaigrette, or as part of a mixed *mezze*.

MEAT PIE
There is nothing extraordinary about this pie. I make it when I feel like something homely to remind myself that the ordinary things we've grown up with and long since discarded can be very good and shouldn't be forgotten. And it's my husband's favourite; he insisted I include it.

8 oz / 225 g shortcrust pastry made from 4 oz / 120 g wholewheat flour, 4 oz / 120 g white flour, 4 oz / 120 g polyunsaturated margarine (or 2 oz /

60 g each of lard and margarine), a pinch of salt and egg or water to bind.

12 oz / 340 g minced cooked beef or lamb, preferably rare or undercooked; 1 carrot, small onion, stick of celery, all finely chopped; ⅓ oz / 10 g beef, mutton fat or butter; 1 dessertspoon of tomato purée; lamb or beef stock as appropriate; 1 scant tablespoon of flour; 2 tablespoons chopped parsley; soy sauce (optional).

Make the pastry in the usual way, either by hand or in a food processor. If you prefer your own pastry mix, use that. Soften the chopped vegetables in a knob of butter or beef or mutton fat as appropriate, and cook until they start to brown. Add the meat, sprinkle in the flour and stir for a couple of minutes. Add the tomato purée and enough stock to moisten but avoid any sloppiness. Cook for 5 minutes, remove from the heat, stir in the parsley, and check the seasoning. Beef tends to give less flavour than lamb; if you find this is so, add a dash of soy sauce. Set aside and allow to cool.

   Line a 7 in / 18 cm flan tin with a thin layer of pastry, making sure the sides are of a good depth. Fill with the meat mixture, cover with the remaining pastry, using some of the trimmings for decoration. Cut a slit in the centre, brush with egg or milk and bake on a baking sheet in a hot oven 220°C / 425°F / gas mark 7 for 15 minutes, then for a further 15 minutes or so at 180°C / 350°F / gas mark 4. In winter serve with potatoes and kale or spring cabbage, in summer with a salad. Any left over makes excellent cold eating.

KIDNEYS IN AN ONION HAT
This is for prize English onions or, at least, very large ones. It is based on an idea first recorded by Nell Heaton in her *Traditional Recipes of the British Isles*.

4 large onions; 4–5 lamb's kidneys, central tubes removed and diced into sizeable pieces; 1–1¼ pints / 600–750 ml lamb or beef stock; 1 dessertspoon potato flour; sherry or madeira; butter; mustard (optional); mace.

Blanch the cleaned but unpeeled onions in boiling water for 7–8 minutes. Drain, trim the root end, remove the skins and slice off the tops about a third of the way down the onion. Hollow out the insides leaving the walls about ½ in / 1¼ cm thick. This is not as easy as it sounds. Chop the pieces of left-over onion finely and set on one side. Put a tiny dab of butter in the base of each onion and fill with diced kidney, seasoned with a little powdered mace, and some of the reserved onion. Add a dessertspoonful of sherry or madeira and replace the lids. Transfer the onions to a shallow ovenproof dish. Soften the left-over onion in a little butter for about 5 minutes and pile round the onions. Pour in enough stock to cover the base to a depth of 1 in / 2.5 cm, bring gently to the boil and transfer to a moderate oven 180°C / 350°F / gas mark 4, lightly covered with foil. Cook for about an hour, or until the onions are soft when tested with a skewer. Remove from the oven, add a small glass of sherry or madeira, a little mustard if liked, and thicken the sauce with the potato flour slaked in water. Serve in the same dish. Good with Brussels sprouts and baked potatoes.

LIVER AND PRUNE COMPOTE
A rather special liver dish, rich and full of goodness. For maximum effect, serve it on a plain white dish.

1 lb /450 g lamb's liver, sliced; 8 oz / 225 g largish prunes; red wine to cover (approx. 8 fl oz / 240 ml); 2 in / 5 cm stick of cinnamon; 2 tablespoons brandy; lemon juice; $\frac{1}{3}$–$\frac{1}{2}$ oz / 10–15 g butter plus 1–2 tablespoons vegetable oil; milk to soak liver; flour to dust.

Prepare the prune purée beforehand or the day before. Cover the prunes with boiling water, leave for a minute and then drain. This helps to remove the mineral oil and preservatives. Transfer to a pan with enough red wine to cover, add the cinnamon and cook gently, covered, for 20–25 minutes until soft. Leave to cool, overnight if you have the time. Fish out the cinnamon, remove the stones and purée in a blender till smooth, diluting with enough water to make a thick, chocolate brown sauce. Return to the pan, stir in the brandy, add lemon juice to sharpen, and set aside until needed.

A couple of hours before you want to eat, soak the liver in milk. Dry, cut into neat strips and dust lightly with flour. Fry briskly for 3–4 minutes. Try not to cook the pieces too long and turn so that each side is nicely browned. Meanwhile reheat the purée. To serve, spread the prune sauce thickly over the base of a serving dish and arrange the slices of liver on top. Accompany with a few noodles, serving any vegetables before or after.

For an even grander dish, use calves' liver. Keep the slices whole and cook very briefly – a minute or so either side – and serve the prune *compote* on the side, reducing the quantity accordingly.

PORK WITH SAGE AND MARSALA

A good combination of flavours and a useful dish for two when time is short. The secret of the dish lies in the stock. It needs to be very concentrated, boiled down to a syrupy glaze.

8 oz / 225 g pork tenderloin, sliced into ¼ in / ½ cm slices, and trimmed of any fat or sinew; 3–4 sage leaves, shredded into thin strips; 3–4 tablespoons marsala and the same of syrupy beef glaze; ⅓ oz / 10 g butter plus scant tablespoon olive oil for frying.

The whole dish takes only 3–4 minutes to cook and is then left while you eat the first course. Cook the pork slices briskly in a heavy pan in which you have melted the fat until very hot, adding the sage half-way through. They will need only a minute each side and you will have to raise the heat slightly to keep them cooking briskly. Remove to a warm plate, deglaze the pan with marsala and bubble till almost reduced. Add enough concentrated meat stock to form just a little syrupy sauce, bearing in mind that the juices from the meat will dilute it down. Return the meat to the pan, heat through and turn the pieces over to coat with the sauce. Taste – it may need an extra dash of either marsala or stock – transfer to a heated serving dish and keep warm, covered, in a low oven or on a warming tray to allow the meat to relax and the juices to mingle with the sauce for a few minutes. Serve with rice. Spinach makes an excellent accompaniment. [Serves 2.]

THAI CRAB AND PORK STEAMED MEAT BALLS

Adapted from Jennifer Brennan's excellent *Thai Cooking*, a good book to turn to when you're tired of European tastes. Don't be put off by the meat and shellfish combination, it works very well. The dip is my own concoction.

6 oz / 170 g each of cooked crab meat and lean, uncooked pork, free from skin and fat; 1 slice of white or light wheatmeal bread, crusts removed and soaked in 2½ fl oz / 75 ml milk; clove of garlic, crushed and chopped; 2 spring onions, finely chopped, including some green; 1 beaten egg; 1 tablespoon chopped coriander.

For decoration: sprigs of coriander; 1 fresh chilli, seeds removed.

For the dipping sauce: 2 tablespoons satay sauce (available from Chinese supermarkets); hot water; 1–2 teaspoons soy sauce.

Grind the pork in a food processor, or mince it finely. Combine all the ingredients in a large bowl and mix thoroughly to a smooth, slightly sticky paste. Cut out 16 rounds of aluminium foil about 2–2½ in / 5–6¼ cm across and place a generous dessertspoonful of mixture in each. Draw the foil around but not over the mixture and pinch the edges to form little silver dishes. When finished they will look like silver flowers with pink centres. Decorate the centre of each with a tiny frond of coriander and a strip of red chilli cut into curls, diamonds or *julienne* strips. Set aside in the refrigerator until needed.

To cook, steam for about 10 minutes or until firm. The exact cooking time depends on the size; try one to check. Serve as they are, pretty and appetising, accompanied by the dipping sauce – the satay paste diluted to a thin cream with hot water and with soy sauce to taste. Eat as a first course or as part of an oriental meal.

CHICKEN IN SALT

This way of cooking chicken produces a beautifully moist bird, tender and of good flavour. The salt forms a hard crust and acts as a hermetic casing, yet the meat is in no way salty. The salt comes away at the end like a baked clay pot and any remaining grains are brushed off to leave a pale golden, nicely plumped bird.

1 fresh chicken, 3½ lb / 1½ kg, trussed; up to 5½ lb / 2½ kg cooking salt.

Spread 2 huge pieces of cooking foil over a roasting tin, overlapping the centres by about 4 in / 10 cm. Cover the base with a good layer of salt 1 in / 2.5 cm thick and sit the chicken on top. Cover the vent with a piece of foil to stop salt from getting into the cavity. Using your arms, draw the foil up loosely round the chicken. Fill with enough salt to completely bury the bird and wrap up tightly, enclosing the mountain of salt. Cook in a very hot oven, 230°C / 450°F / gas mark 8, for 1½ hours. Remove from the oven and fold back the foil to reveal the hardened crust. Bang the whole thing down on a working surface – drastic but effective. Remove the pieces of broken crust, ease out the chicken very gently, transfer to a dish and brush off any remaining salt with a good thick brush, a paintbrush, for example. Serve the chicken surrounded by watercress and accompany with saffron rice or new potatoes and salad.

Chicken prepared this way lends itself to sauces and relishes of all kinds. I generally serve a simple garlic purée let down with creamy milk or single cream (see p. 70). Fruit and citrus *compotes* served on the side are excellent. At cherry time, Mrs Leyel's cherry salad – stoned fresh cherries, lightly sprinkled with sugar, a dash of brandy, a few drops of oil and a little finely chopped tarragon and chervil – is delicious.

If need be, the chicken can be kept in its silvery cocoon for 15–20 minutes or so. Remove from the oven and leave undisturbed on the side until the time comes to serve. Any untainted salt can be stored for future use.

JAMBONNEAUX

A dish with a charming name, from Prue Leith's Cookery School. It takes a little time but is worth it. Stuffings can be varied to suit. If you intend serving the *Jambonneaux* cold, it's no more trouble to choose two different stuffings and serve the meat sliced to show off the contrasting centres.

4 large chicken legs.

For the stuffing: 4 oz / 120 g minced ham; 4 oz / 120 g lightly cooked chicken livers; scant teaspoon chopped tarragon; ½ oz / 15 g softened butter cut into tiny pieces.

For the sauce and cooking: *mirepoix* of finely chopped onion, carrot and celery; ¾ pint / 425 ml light chicken stock; 4–5 tablespoons madeira; bay leaf; ⅓ oz / 10 g butter plus 2 tablespoons vegetable oil for frying; a little potato flour.

Prepare each leg in the same way. Chop through the ball and socket joint at the foot and discard the end bit which can go for stock. Starting from the thigh end, with a sharp knife carefully scrape away the flesh from the bone, folding it back as you go along. Work round the knee joint and continue down the leg until all the bone has been exposed. It can then be removed, leaving a roughly triangular shaped piece of flesh with a hole running down the centre. The whole operation sounds more complicated than it is; a little practice and it shouldn't take more than 3–4 minutes. Be careful not to pierce the flesh through to the outside skin, so keep the knife as close to the bone as possible. Mix the stuffing ingredients until thoroughly blended and fill the cavities. With a large sewing needle and fine thread, sew each leg up the side and along the top, keeping the stitches loose to allow for expansion during cooking. Sew the foot end also. Each leg now resembles a miniature ham – hence the name 'little hams'. This can be done in advance and the legs left in the refrigerator until later.

Melt the butter and the oil in a heavy frying pan and brown the chicken legs lightly on each side. Remove and set aside. Add the chopped vegetables to the pan and cook gently for 10 minutes or so, stirring frequently, until they take colour and are beginning to brown. Replace the chicken legs, pour over the madeira, previously warmed in a ladle or small pan. Set alight and give the pan a shake to distribute the flames. Add the stock and bay leaf, cover and simmer for about 50 minutes, or until the juices from the meat run clear when pierced with a skewer. Remove the chicken and keep warm. Strain the sauce, pressing hard against the sieve to extract the juices from the vegetables. Skim off the fat and boil down to concentrate the flavour. Correct the seasoning if necessary, and thicken with a suspicion of potato flour slaked in water. Remove the threads from the *jambonneaux* and arrange on a serving dish. Garnish with watercress and serve the sauce separately, along with a potato purée and a few crisp beans. Alternatively serve cold with jacket potatoes as a part of a salad meal. This way, one *jambonneau* will be sufficient for two. Save the sauce, unthickened, for another dish.

CHICKEN PIQUANT
A marvellously easy dish. Very fresh, and beautifully summery. Use the best and reddest tomatoes you can find.

4 chicken breasts; 1½ lb / 675 g fresh tomatoes; small onion, chopped as fine as possible; 1 tablespoon chopped tarragon; 2 fl oz / 60 ml white wine vinegar; ½ oz / 15 g butter plus 1–2 tablespoons vegetable oil for frying.

Skin the tomatoes by plunging them into boiling water for a minute. Quarter, remove the seeds and cut each quarter into 3–4 strips and set aside. Melt the butter in a frying pan which will hold the chicken breasts comfortably and add enough oil to cover the base of the pan. Dry the chicken breasts on kitchen paper and lightly brown on both sides, keeping them moving with a palette knife to prevent them from sticking. Add the onion previously chopped almost to a purée and soften for a minute or so. Pour in the vinegar, turn up the heat slightly and cook briskly until it has all but evaporated. Add the tomatoes, reduce the heat, cover and continue to cook gently until the juices from the chicken run clear, 10–15 minutes.

Transfer the chicken to a serving dish and keep warm. Turn the heat up briefly to reduce any wateriness from the sauce, stir in the tarragon and spoon around but not over the chicken. Decorate each breast with a single leaf of tarragon and serve immediately with plain rice and a green salad.

SPICED CHICKEN (OR LAMB) PILAFF

6–8 oz / 170–225 g left-over diced chicken or lamb; 8 oz / 225 g basmati rice; 10 fl oz / scant 300 ml chicken stock or water; 1 large onion sliced; fresh chilli, seeded and chopped; ½ green pepper, de-seeded and cut into strips; 4–6 dried apricots, diced into small pieces; 1–2 tablespoons pine kernels; ½ teaspoon ground allspice or 6 berries lightly toasted and crushed in a mortar; pinch of salt; 1 tablespoon fresh coriander; ⅓–½ oz / 10–15 g butter, oil or ghee for frying.

Choose a large, heavy frying pan and sweat the onion, pepper and chilli for 15–20 minutes until soft and cooked through. Keep the lid on, the heat low, and stir from time to time. Stir in the apricots, pine kernels and allspice. At this stage the pilaff can be left and the cooking completed later. Wash the rice in several changes of water and leave to soak for half an hour. Drain through a sieve and set aside.

To complete the cooking, raise the heat slightly and stir in the drained rice, turning it over and over until it becomes impregnated with the juices from the vegetables and takes on a translucent sheen. Distribute the meat lightly over the top, pour in the stock or water, add a pinch of salt and bring to the boil. Cover and cook gently for 5–7 minutes until the stock has been absorbed. Turn off the heat and leave for another 10 minutes for the flavours to develop. Carefully turn out into a heated serving dish, sprinkle with coriander, and serve immediately with a green or cucumber salad and a bowl of plain yoghurt. This quantity should serve 2–4.

Lamb can toughen when reheated. If you prefer, add it towards the end of cooking, giving it time just to heat through.

CHICKEN LIVER PARFAIT

This is a cross between a pâté and a mousse. It has the advantages of both but is lighter on calories than either. Serves 6–8 as a first course.

approx. 10 oz / 280 g chicken livers; 4 oz / 120 g *quark*; 4 fl oz / 120 ml single cream; 3–4 tablespoons madeira, port or sweetish sherry; 2 eggs; milk.

Cut away any stringy or greenish bits from the livers and allow them to soak in milk for a couple of hours. Drain and blend with the other ingredients in a food processor or blender until absolutely smooth and mousse-like. Pour into a lightly oiled mould allowing 1 in / 2.5 cm or so headspace for the pâté to rise during cooking. (This, alas, is a temporary benefit, the pâté ungraciously shrinks on cooling.) Bake in a very low oven, 130°C / 265°F / gas mark ½, for 2–2½ hours until the pâté feels firm to the touch and the juices run clear when pierced with a skewer. Allow to cool and serve as a first course with toast. Wrapped in cling film, it will keep for up to a week in the refrigerator.

MAJOR POLLARD'S PLANKED PARTRIDGES

Two books on game cookery stand out above all others. The first is Julia Drysdale's *Classic Game Cookery*, published in 1975, the second Major Hugh Pollard's *The Sportsman's Cookery Book* of 1926. His recipes are not always to modern tastes, nor does he claim any culinary expertise, but his book makes compulsive reading. This is his method, in his own words, for cooking fish or game on a plank of seasoned wood.

PLANKED PARTRIDGE

'Plank cookery is almost unknown in this country, but it is an ideal method of cooking both fish and fowl of delicate savour ... Its peculiarity is that it restores to foods that valuable and delightful flavour which food of all kinds cooked on an open wood fire acquires from the fuel used.

A plank simply consists of a piece of seasoned oak board, 1½ or 2 inches thick. This should be trimmed oval or rounded cornered to fit a largish dish ... rub it all over with olive oil and put it in a hot oven till it is slightly browned; season it again with olive oil a second and third time and it is fit to use. Note well that a cooking plank is never to be washed. To clean it simply scrape and rub with paper; it should be kept in a paper when not in use ... the more you cook on a plank the better it gets ...'

Split the partridge down the back, rub it with oil and beat it flat. Heat the plank in the oven, place the bird on it, securing with tacks. Cook in the lower part of a hot oven for 20 minutes. Baste occasionally with melted butter. Or use under the grill. Fish should be tacked down in the same way. Other woods such as beech or cherry can be used. Serve the food on the plank which also keeps it hot.

ROAST PHEASANT WITH BURST ORANGES

A pheasant is a deceptively economical bird. The ratio of breast meat to other meat is very high and unless your pheasant is very small, one bird should feed four. The hen pheasant is said to be sweeter than the cock but I cannot honestly say I find much difference. The cock is larger and has less of the yellow fat which I do not care for and prefer to remove, for it seems to give the meat next to it an unpleasant tang.

1 hen or cock pheasant; thin strips of fatty unsmoked bacon; sprigs of thyme; ½ oz / 15 g butter plus another ½ oz / 15 g, melted, for basting.

For the stuffing (optional): 1 oz / 30 g bulgur; 1 tablespoon raisins soaked in 1–2 tablespoons brandy; small chopped onion; knob of butter.

For the sauce: juice of 1 large Seville orange plus extra juice if necessary; 1 tablespoon Seville marmalade; 3–4 fl oz / 90–120 ml white wine; well flavoured game stock; 6–8 clementines or tangerines; 1 teaspoon of potato flour slaked in water.

To make the stuffing, soak the raisins, overnight if possible, in the brandy. Soak the bulgur in water in the usual way and then drain, pressing out all the excess moisture. Soften the onion in a knob of butter, mix with the wheat, raisins and any remaining brandy and set aside till needed.

Rub the pheasant with butter and cover the breast and legs with fatty bacon. Lightly fill the cavity with the stuffing or, alternatively, put a generous knob of butter inside the bird. Truss well, put on its side in a roasting tin, surround with a few sprigs of thyme and roast in a hot oven, 200°C / 400°F / gas mark 6, or a little higher, for about 40–60 minutes. As a general rule allow 20 minutes to the pound, plus 10 minutes. Baste with butter from time to time. Half way through turn the bird on to its other side. Towards the end of the cooking remove the bacon. Transfer it to another pan and crisp in the oven. Baste the pheasant with the Seville marmalade and orange juice. Remove and keep warm, breast side down, while you finish the sauce.

Each bird will roast a little differently. All game should be well basted, as often as you can. I have found it almost impossible to have both the breast and legs ready at the same time. If I can, I concentrate on the breast and save the legs for another meal, which means a slightly shorter overall cooking time. The legs are cooked when the juices run clear. An alternative is to cook the bird until the breast is done and then to detach the legs and finish them separately.

While the pheasant is cooking prepare the oranges. Put them in a pan, cover with cold water, bring to the boil and blanch for 5 minutes. Drain and transfer to a shallow dish with a little water in the pan, cover lightly with a piece of dampened greaseproof paper and cook in the oven for 25–35 minutes or until they're soft and almost bursting.

Discard the thyme and remove the fat from the pan juices. Set over a moderate heat, pour in the wine, bubble up and reduce by half, scraping all the bits from the bottom of the pan. Add enough stock to make up to a generous 15 fl oz / 450 ml and cook until the sauce is of a good flavour. Taste and adjust seasoning with extra orange juice or marmalade if necessary, though aim for a well-balanced flavour, slightly tart and not obsessively orangey. Thicken very slightly with some of the potato flour slaked in water.

Serve the pheasant garnished with burst oranges and watercress, handing the sauce separately, adding any juices which have run from the pheasant while it's been resting. Or take the meat off the bone, arrange in a handsome serving dish, moisten with some of the sauce, and garnish as before. Accompany the pheasant with the bacon, broken into bits and served in a small bowl, and fanned potatoes. A slightly bitter endive salad, or spinach, and a few chestnut croquettes finish the dish in style.

PHEASANT STUFFED WITH VENISON

This grew out of a suggestion made to me by Phil Hyde who runs a fishmonger's and game shop in Ilkley. It's a festive dish, a variation on the pheasant *normand* theme. You will need to choose a large bird as the breast meat only is served. The legs should go for pâté (see p. 110), or devilled for a mid-week meal, served with rice and salad.

1 large roasting pheasant, 2¼–2½ lb / generous 1 kg in weight when trussed; 6 oz / 170 g venison sausage (approx. 2 thick sausages); 4 juniper berries, crushed and finely chopped; 3–4 tablespoons brandy or calvados; 8 fl oz / 240 ml game or well flavoured chicken stock; 2–4 fl oz / 60–120 ml single cream; 2 medium Cox's apples; 1 teaspoon potato flour slaked in a little water; knob of butter and 1 dessertspoon mild olive oil for frying the pheasant, plus another extra knob of butter for frying the apples.

Remove the skins from the sausages, mash with the juniper berries and then lightly stuff the cavity with this mixture. Melt the butter and oil in a heavy casserole dish which will hold the pheasant snugly and brown the bird on all sides. Warm a small ladleful (2 tablespoons) of brandy or calvados, pour over the pheasant and flame. Once the flames have died down, turn the pheasant on its side, pour over the stock and bring gently to the boil. Cover with buttered paper, put the lid on and transfer to a moderate oven, 180°C / 350°F / gas mark 4, for 40–45 minutes, turning the bird on to its other side half way through. Remove the pheasant and dig out the stuffing with a spoon. Return the pheasant to a low oven to relax and keep warm, protected with its buttered paper, while you attend to the rest of the dish.

Start with the sauce. Skim off all the fat from the braising liquid, reduce a little to concentrate the flavour and then add cream to soften as you see fit. Cook a little longer and then set aside. Next the garnish. Dice the stuffing into bite-sized knobs and fry over a moderate heat in an ungreased pan until appetisingly brown and crisp. This will take a good 5–7 minutes. Transfer to a dish, scraping up the bits and keep warm in the oven. Peel, core and quarter the apples, slicing each quarter into three. Melt another knob of butter in a small shallow pan and gently fry the apple slices over a fairly moderate flame for about 5 minutes, until just soft and beginning to turn golden. Finish with the rest of the brandy or calvados, turning the heat up slightly to evaporate the alcohol. Transfer to the oven to keep warm.

For the final assembly, drain off into the sauce all the juices which will have run from the pheasant. Carve the breast into fine, handsome slices and arrange in a hot serving dish. Reheat the sauce, check the final taste and bind very slightly with no more than a suspicion of potato flour. Spoon the sauce over the pheasant – there should be just enough to moisten it nicely – and garnish with a border of alternate slices of venison and apple. Serve with *pommes nature* (see p. 79) and a few chestnuts, cooked as described on p. 67, and finished by frying briefly in a knob of butter to make them glisten. A salad to start with and fruit or perhaps a tea cream to follow.

PIGEONS AGRODOLCE

A rather special recipe, for the unspecial pigeon. It was one of Hannah Glasse's recipes (she has twenty-four) which first persuaded me that pigeons are worth cooking. She wrapped her pigeons in pastry and boiled them in a cloth: 'they eat exceeding good and nice, and will yield Sauce enough of a very agreeable Relish'. This, by contrast, is an entirely modern affair. The stock needs to be made in advance but the dish itself takes no more than 30 minutes to cook.

4 pigeons; 2 tablespoons brandy; 2 tablespoons wine vinegar; 1 tablespoon sugar; ½ oz / 15 g butter plus 1 tablespoon vegetable oil for frying.

For the stock: 1 leek, carrot, onion and stick of celery; 5 fl oz / 150 ml red wine; peppercorns, bay leaf, sprig of thyme; large piece of pork rind or a well-washed pigs trotter; knob of butter and oil for frying.

To finish: 1 teaspoon potato flour; ½ oz / 15 g butter, cut into pieces; 4 oz / 120 g black grapes, halved and seeded.

Cut the breasts from the pigeons and remove the silvery tendon which runs along the length of the underside by gently inserting a sharp knife and scraping the tendon away from the flesh. Set aside in the refrigerator until needed. Next make the stock. Sweat the sliced vegetables and broken-up pigeon carcasses in a little oil and butter until well browned. Take your time and keep the heat low. Add all the other ingredients, cover with generous 4 pints / 2½ l of water, bring to the boil, skim, and simmer for 3–4 hours until the broth has reduced by half. Alternatively cook for 45 minutes at high pressure in a pressure cooker, adding enough water to come half way up the pan. Strain the stock, take off all the fat and set aside.

For the final cooking, brown the pigeon breasts quickly on both sides in butter and oil. Drain off any remaining fat and pour over a good measure of warmed brandy. Ignite and shake the pan until the flames have died down. (Flaming is simple enough and usually spectacular, but should be approached with due caution, so keep a lid handy.) Completely cover the pigeon breasts with stock and gently poach for 10–12 minutes. Do not overcook them: they should still be slightly pink inside. Remove the breasts and keep warm in the oven while you finish the sauce. Have the caramel ready, previously prepared by boiling the sugar in a small pan with a tablespoon of water. Watch it carefully once it starts to turn – it will take only a few seconds. Leave it to cool a little and stir in the wine vinegar. Reheat, if necessary, to dissolve the caramel in the vinegar and set aside until needed.

Add the caramel to the poaching liquid and boil down vigorously to produce about 15 fl oz / 450 ml of liquid, tasting frequently. The sauce should be rich and of a good flavour, neither sweet nor sour but with definite piquancy. Allow to cool a little and lightly bind with a little potato flour slaked in water. Finish by whisking in the butter off the heat, which gives extra body and a lovely sheen. Cover a handsome serving dish with the sauce. Lay the pigeon breasts on top, herring-bone fashion, and decorate with the black grapes previously warmed through in the oven. Serve with rice or chocolate pasta.

BRAISED GAME WITH RASPBERRIES

The slightly tart sweetness of raspberries makes them a natural partner for game, especially smaller birds cooked whole in their own juices. Their colour, too, adds a cheerful note.

per person: 1 small game bird – teal, woodcock, snipe, quail; approx. 1 tablespoon raspberries (frozen are fine); 1 tablespoon brandy; 2–3 tablespoons concentrated game stock; extra raspberries for decoration; few drops of raspberry vinegar; clarified butter or butter and oil for frying.

Brown the birds slowly and evenly in a heavy casserole. Remove from the pan and drain off all the fat. Lightly stuff the cavities with raspberries, return the birds to the pan and pour over the brandy. Cook for a minute or two over a fierce heat until most of the brandy has evaporated. Turn down to the lowest heat possible, moisten with stock, cover with greaseproof paper and jam the lid on tight. Cook for about 35–45 minutes – the exact cooking time will depend on your bird – until the juices run clear. Transfer the birds to a serving dish, garnish with a few extra raspberries taken from a bottle of raspberry liqueur and keep warm.

You should have a small amount of dark and deliciously-flavoured sauce. Take off any surface fat, add a few drops of raspberry vinegar to heighten the flavour, spoon over the birds and serve. Bread croûtes are an obvious accompaniment, but you will need no vegetables for this dish. For safety, go for plain rice; for style – and flavour – go for chocolate pasta.

For a change, a couple of previously-cooked tablespoons of wheat grains mixed with the raspberries add a pleasant chewiness to the stuffing. The carcasses should go for consommé.

GAME PÂTÉ

Another lean-line pâté but, this time, one in the classic mould, useful for left-overs and small quantities of game.

4–6 oz / 120–170 g each of left-over, undercooked or raw game and lean belly pork; 8 oz / 225 g chicken livers; 1 large egg; slice of white or light wheatmeal bread soaked in game stock or milk; clove of garlic, mashed and finely chopped; slice of lean, unsmoked bacon, fat removed; 4 juniper berries, crushed and finely chopped; 2 tablespoons brandy; black pepper (optional).

This quantity will fill a container 3 in / 7.5 cm deep and 4 in / 10 cm wide of 1 pint / 600 ml capacity and will serve 4–6.

Take off the pork rind, cut away most of the fat and slice the meat roughly. Put the pork, bacon, half the game and the egg and the bread squeezed dry of excess moisture into a food processor and process until smooth. If you have no processor, mince the meats finely and beat thoroughly with the other ingredients. Turn the mixture into a bowl. Dice the rest of the game and roughly chop the chicken livers, remembering to discard any greenish bits. If you have any liver from the game and its strong taste is to your liking, add this also. Add remaining ingredients, mix thoroughly and leave for a couple of hours to allow the flavours to develop, or longer if it suits. Transfer the pâté to a buttered container, cover with greaseproof or a butter paper and cook in a pan of hot water in a moderate oven, 180°C / 350°F / gas mark 4, for about 1½ hours, until the juices run clear when tested with a skewer and the pâté has begun to shrink from the sides. Cool, weight and keep in the refrigerator for a couple of days to mellow before serving.

Fish

What do we mean by 'cooking' a fish?

We all know the answer, in practical terms, to this question. But it is worth knowing the scientific answer. To cook a fish is to raise its temperature, by which I mean the temperature of its innermost parts, to about 145°F (63°C). Doing this brings about the various changes which characterize cooked fish. It is pointless, and in fact detracts from the quality of your dish, to raise the temperature higher or to keep it at that height for a long time.

It follows from the preceding paragraph that cooking time must depend on the greatest thickness of the fish. Heat travels gradually from the outside to the inside. The further it has to go, the longer it takes.

However, the time taken does not vary in simple proportion to the thickness, but in proportion to the square of the thickness. This principle, of course, applies to other substances, not just to fish; but many people are unaware of it. If it takes 2 minutes to cook a piece of fish 2 cm thick, then a piece 4 cm thick will require 8 minutes, not 4 minutes.

ALAN DAVIDSON *North Atlantic Seafood*, 1979

Fish is, without doubt, one of nature's perfect foods. As yet, it is largely unsoiled by man. We should take advantage of it when we can.

Fresh fish makes fine eating; grill it or poach it and serve with savoury butters or with the juices softened with a little cream. More robust fish lend themselves to onion-based stews, lightly spiced pilaffs, savoury stuffings and often combine well with fruit. The more delicate make fragile dumplings and light mousses. Potted fish is a quick and easy starter. Cold fish makes lovely salads. Shellfish add colour and the taste of the sea.

Fish stocks

'It is the work of half an hour, yet it will be the instantly available basis for fish soup, a fish stew, a liquor in which to cook your fish to great advantage, the main ingredient for a fish velouté for your sauces and the ideal basis for cooking mussels. It is madness not to make it.'

So writes Tom Jaine in his book Fish Times Thirty. His instructions for fish stock are simple, and to the point.

'Skin, bone and trimmings from the fish you have bought that day, or supplied by the fishmonger from his own debris after preparing fillets. 1 onion, 2 pieces of celery, 2 carrots, bay leaves, peppercorns, thyme, dill and parsley stalks.

Peel, wash and coarsely slice the vegetables. Put them in a pot with the fish trimmings and the herbs. Cover with cold water and bring to a gentle boil. Simmer for half an hour, strain through a fine sieve and put to cool.'

Any fish can be used to make a fish stock except the oily or smoked kind and, generally speaking, the finer the fish the finer the stock. The debris from shellfish (see p. 34) makes excellent stocks for use as a base for soups or accompanying sauces. Herbs are useful but should be used cautiously and sparingly. For general purposes, parsley, bay leaves and maybe a little thyme, especially lemon thyme, or fennel produce the best results. A glass of wine, a spoonful of wine vinegar or a little lemon juice all make good (and, I find, necessary) additions to the basic mix. Once the stock has been strained, boiling it down produces a concentrated essence or fish *fumet* which, used in small quantities, gives body and flavour to sauces or soups.

A SIMPLE WAY TO COOK FISH

Preheat the oven to 230°C / 450°F / gas mark 8. Clean the fish, lay in a greased pan, dot with shavings of butter and moisten with a little white wine, no more than half a glass. If wine is not available, use water and a squeeze of lemon juice instead. Cover and cook for anything from 10–15 minutes for small and flat fish to about 25 minutes or so for larger or thick fish. The fish is cooked when the flesh next to the backbone parts easily with a knife. Serve with a few boiled potatoes. For additional sauces see pp. 115–117.

CHARCOAL GRILLED FISH

Fish grilled over charcoal acquires a rare succulence. Any type of fish can be cooked this way, from the finest scallops to the humble farm-fed trout. For whole fish a double sided, fish-shaped grill to hold the fish is essential, otherwise it can end up a messy business with most of the fish dropping through on to the charcoal. These grills also do for fish steaks. Clean the fish, score the flesh diagonally at its thickest part, brush with olive oil, squeeze over a few drops of lemon juice and set aside. The cavities can be stuffed with fresh herbs or left bare. If you wish, lay a branch of fennel along the length of both sides of the grill, slipping the fish in between the branches. The grill will hold the fennel in place which will char deliciously as the fish cooks. Should fresh sardines or red mullet be available, wrap them in blanched vine leaves and baste with olive oil. The humbler, but in no way to be despised, herring is also delicious done this way.

Fish should be cooked slowly, 3–4 in / 7.5–10 cm above the coals. Turn them once or twice. Small fish will take 5–10 minutes, moderately sized fish 10–15 minutes and larger fish longer. Bear in mind that it's the thickness that counts rather than the overall weight.

Sauces for charcoal grilled fish can be as varied as you want, though they should not be copious or detract from the essential flavour of food cooked over charcoal. For white fish, a pat of savoury butter makes a simple and excellent accompaniment; for salmon, trout or halibut, something like sorrel and mustard sauce or walnut and horseradish sauce (see below); for more robust flavoured fish, try a *rouille*, *pesto*, or a fresh tomato relish made by roughly chopping ripe, skinned and deseeded tomatoes with a mixture of finely chopped parsley, basil or fennel, and moistened with a few drops of olive oil.

A FEW SAUCES FOR FISH

Sauce rouille
Rouille is a splendid, garlicky concoction from Provence, an excellent sauce which combines pungency with sweetness. It's perfect for charcoal grilled fish, for spreading on dry, baked-hard bread to float in fish soups, to add to fish stews, and to add an unauthentic touch to egg dishes or chakchouka (see p. 144). Recipes vary quite infuriatingly. Red peppers, oil and garlic, all pounded together, seem to be – but are not always – the constant ingredients. Chillies, egg yolks and, occasionally, saffron also appear. This is the recipe I use, based on the one given in *Mediterranean Seafood* by Alan Davidson whose own source was the great father of Provençal cookery J. B. Reboul.

1 red pepper, quartered and seeds removed; small slice of white bread, crusts removed; large clove of garlic, crushed; 1 tablespoon olive oil; few spoonfuls of fish broth or water; salt (optional).

Arrange the quartered pepper, skin side uppermost on a heat-proof dish and grill under a fairly fierce heat until the surface of the skin is blackened. This preliminary grilling softens the pepper and brings out its delicious sweetness. Wash under running water and rub off the skins. Chop coarsely and set aside. Meanwhile soak the bread in water and squeeze out the excess moisture. Put the pepper, garlic and bread in a blender or food processor and process until smooth. Scrape the paste into a bowl and stir in the olive oil. You should now have a thick, homogenous paste. Taste to see if any salt is required and set aside until needed.

Just before serving, let down with a little fish broth to give the desired consistency – I like to keep it very thick but there are no hard and fast rules, so be guided by taste and what you want the sauce for. If no fish broth is available, let down with water which gives a fresher taste some may prefer. This produces a smooth sauce. For a lumpier texture make in the traditional way and pound by hand in a mortar. It's more work and I've yet to be convinced of its merits. Sufficient for 3–4 small servings.

Sorrel and Mustard Sauce
Chop a large handful of young sorrel leaves to a purée, removing the central midrib stalk first. Add a teaspoon of mild mustard and 2–3 tablespoons of thick sour cream. Use as a relish. An excellent little sauce

for salmon, salmon trout, or veal chops cooked on the barbecue. Sufficient for 2–3.

Dill and Cucumber Cream

Drain about 15 fl oz / 425 ml of yoghurt until it is very thick. Transfer to a bowl, add 2–3 tablespoons of single cream and whip until smooth and creamy. Meanwhile skin and remove the seeds from about a quarter of a cucumber. Coarsely grate the flesh, transfer to a sieve and gently press out all the excess juice. Lightly mix into the cream together with some finely chopped dill and one or two drops of vinegar. Pile into a bowl, decorate with a little more finely chopped dill and serve as a sauce for hot or cold salmon or to accompany a fish mousse. The amount of cucumber and other seasonings can be varied to suit, but aim always for a thick rather than a sloppy sauce.

Based on a similar sauce given in Tom Jaine's *Fish Times Thirty*.

TWO HORSERADISH SAUCES

Mr Gladstone's recipe from Ireland (1870s)

From *Good Cook Sauces, Sweet and Savoury* by Lady Muriel Beckwith. I have altered the proportions slightly to give a less sharp sauce.

2 hard-boiled egg yolks; 2 heaped tablespoons freshly grated horseradish; 1 tablespoon tarragon vinegar; 1–2 teaspoons caster sugar; 1–2 tablespoons double or single cream; extra vinegar (optional).

Work the egg yolks to a smooth paste with the vinegar, adding it gradually. Beat in all the other ingredients, finally adding enough cream to form a cohesive, soft paste. Check and make any adjustments to seasoning – a little more sugar or vinegar perhaps – and serve with smoked fish in small heaped yellow domes on the side of the plate. Sufficient for 3–4 small servings.

Walnut and Horseradish Sauce

A lighter version of Escoffier's classic, as given by Elizabeth David in her *French Provincial Cooking*. Escoffier's sauce calls for ¼ pint / 150 ml double cream, which adds 650 calories. This version decreases the fat content considerably, increases the protein value slightly and adds only 250 calories.

Remove the skins from 2 oz / 60 g shelled walnuts by pouring boiling water over them and picking the skins off when they become cool enough to handle. Chop *very* finely and set aside. Drain 5 fl oz / 150 ml of yoghurt until it is thick and reduced by about a half. Mix with the same quantity of single cream, beating thoroughly. Lightly mix in the walnuts and 2 tablespoons of fresh, finely grated horseradish. Finally add 1–2 teaspoons of sugar and lemon juice, both to taste. Serve with salmon and other fine fish. Sufficient for 4 small servings.

STAR-FISH SALAD

Prawn cocktail apart, we tend to ignore fish as an element in salads. A pity; its softness offers an agreeable contrast to the crispness of the salad ingredients. This is a very pretty salad, clean and fresh tasting. It may sound like a lot of work, but it can all be done in advance. The final assembly is then no more than 3 or 4 minutes' pleasant diversion.

8 oz / 225 g (allow 12 oz / 340 g uncooked weight) diced monkfish, or other firm fish of quality; 4 oz / 120 g finely shredded Chinese cabbage; 4 oz / 120 g fennel, cut into thin strips and diced into lengths around 1 in / 2.5 cm; 1 teaspoon finely scissored chives.

For the dressing: finely grated rind and juice of 1 lime or ½ lemon; 1 tablespoon wine vinegar; 1 tablespoon hot water; 1–2 teaspoons sugar.

For the decoration: strips of smoked salmon; 4 slices of kiwi fruit; 16 mussels (optional) and 1 glass white wine, parsley and shallot/onion to cook them in.

Begin by lightly poaching the fish in a previously prepared and cooled *court-bouillon* made from the fish trimmings, a glass of wine if possible, and the usual seasonings. Saving the stock for soup, drain the fish and add to the cabbage, fennel and herbs. Make the dressing by combining all four ingredients and stirring until the sugar has dissolved. Taste to check the seasoning – it should be sweet but not over so. Pour the dressing over the salad and lightly mix everything together. Cover and chill for a couple of hours.

Next prepare the mussels. Scrub and remove the beards, discarding any that do not shut when tapped sharply with the back of a knife. Set them over a moderate heat with a glass of white wine, chopped parsley and shallot or a little onion, cover and cook for 3–5 minutes, shaking the pan from time to time. Pour into a colander, reserving the juice. Discard any mussels which have refused to open and remove the top half of each shell, leaving the mussels sitting in the bottom half. Set aside until needed.

Arrange the salad mixture in the centre of individual serving plates, mounding it slightly in the middle. Place a slice of kiwi fruit, cut crosswise, in the middle and arrange strips of smoked salmon radiating outwards from it, like the arms of a star-fish. Surround each salad with 4 of the mussels, spooning a little of the reserved liquor into each shell — the remainder should go for soup.

The mussels are an optional extra and look stunning. If you can't be bothered with them, or do not care for them, include a few prawns in the basic mixture, and decorate with extra prawns, additional half slices of kiwi fruit arranged around the border of the salad, or even a few primrose flowers, if it's the right time of year.

MALAYAN MELON AND PRAWNS

A cool, soothing first course, somewhere between a soup and a starter.

2 small ripe melons, cut in half horizontally; 4–6 oz / 120–170 g shelled prawns; 2 tablespoons desiccated coconut; 5 fl oz / 150 ml water; 1 teaspoon mild curry powder; 1 dessertspoon cornflour; 1–2 teaspoons coconut cream; approx 2½ fl oz / 75 ml single cream.

First make the coconut milk. Put the desiccated coconut into a small pan with the water, bring to the boil and allow to cool. Strain the liquid, pressing the debris hard against the sieve to extract the maximum amount of juice from the coconut. Put the coconut liquor back into the pan, stir in the cornflour and curry powder, bring to the boil stirring constantly and simmer for 5 minutes or so, stirring frequently. It should be as thick as *sauce béchamel* and pale yellow in colour. Add coconut cream to taste and allow to cool.

Scoop the seeds from the melons into a sieve set over a bowl to catch the juice. Remove the flesh as neatly as you can and dice into small cubes, again reserving any juice. Save any odd pieces for soups or salads. Add to the coconut mixture the reserved melon juice, most of the prawns chopped into dice, and the melon cubes, together with enough single cream to dilute to a sauce-like consistency. It should not be too thin. Spoon into the melon shells and chill slightly. Just before serving garnish with the reserved prawns. A little grated lime and lime juice makes a pleasant addition; add a twist of lime as decoration.

AN OLD MAID'S CRAB SALAD

'I shall half fill the bowl with cool watercress and lettuce; then, having broken my crab's claws with discrimination, I shall lay dainty fragments of the "meat" atop my greenery. Two kinds of leafage is sufficient; too many flavours, a mistake.

Next, keeping a watchful eye on "deaf ears" (are they its ears and is it deaf!) I shall remove the jaw-part from my crustacean, the better to make a dressing in the shell. To this I shall put a teaspoon of salt, a saltspoon of pepper, and a tablespoon each of vinegar and olive oil. If I have chilli vinegar I shall use no mustard. If this condiment is plain, a teaspoonful of made mustard will give my dressing zest. When it is properly blended, I shall pour it into the bowl and toss all lightly.

Lastly, I shall place slices of hard-boiled egg on my crab salad, and if my marigolds are flowering then, alternate circles of the blooms and thin cucumber rings.

For marigolds *should* be present at the last rites of the crab that meets its end in a salad – for all to gaze upon, and not to eat.'

FLORENCE WHITE *Flowers as Food*, 1934

SMOKED SALMON WITH AGATES OF AVOCADO

A dish in the style of *nouvelle cuisine* which leaves tastes separate but complementary.

6–8 oz / 170–225 g smoked salmon.

For the agates: 1 ripe avocado; approx. 4 oz / 120 g ricotta cheese; rind and juice of 1 lime.

To finish: tiny sprigs of chervil; 4 black olives; slices of lemon.

Scrub the lime in hot water, grate the rind very finely and put both the juice and rind into a blender or food processor. Add the avocado flesh, scraping the green part from under the skin and adding that as well, and blend to a smooth purée. Try and work quickly before the avocado has a chance to discolour – once it has been incorporated with the lime juice you're safe. Sieve the ricotta cheese and blend with the avocado purée to form a velvety smooth but stiff paste. Chill until required in a bowl covered with cling film but don't make it too long before you need it.

To assemble the dish, spread the slices of salmon on individual serving plates, overlapping the sides and tucking in the edges to follow the contours of the plate. The idea is to cover the plate with a pink blush of salmon, leaving a rim of about 2 in / 5 cm around the edge. Shape the avocado mixture into small oval agates, using two teaspoons as you would for *quenelles*. Arrange three in the centre of each plate, like three delicate sepals and place a single black olive in the middle. Decorate the edges with tiny fronds of chervil and slices of lemon, and serve immediately. Offer thinly-sliced brown bread and butter curls separately. A lovely first course to start a formal meal.

CAVEACH OF SOLE, A MODERN WAY
Raw fish is no longer viewed with the same mistrust or trepidation as was the case a few years ago. In any case, in all these and similar recipes the fish does 'cook', not by heat this is true, but by the action of the marinade. This is a mild and delicate version. Thoroughly recommended.

12 oz / 340 g very fresh lemon sole, skinned and filleted; 6 tablespoons dry, white wine; 2 tablespoons lemon juice; 2 tablespoons orange juice; 2 tablespoons walnut oil; large bay leaf broken into bits; scant 1 in / 2.5 cm piece of the white part of a leek; large pinch of saffron; ½ teaspoon salt; few wisps of lemon and orange rind.

Divide the sole into neat strips and lay in a shallow dish. Mix all the liquid ingredients, the saffron and salt, and pour over the fillets. Scatter the finely chopped leek and broken bay leaves over the top, mixing them in lightly and finish with a very few shavings of rind. Cover with cling film and leave in the refrigerator for 24 hours, turning the fish occasionally. The fish is ready when it becomes opaque. This only takes 6–8 hours, but the flavour of the dish reaches perfection at 24 hours. It can be left longer, for up to 48 hours, but the caveach loses some of its delicacy and therefore some of its charm. Serve distributed between 4 plates with a little of the marinade spooned over and triangles of plain dark rye bread to accompany.

POTTED FISH AND FISH PASTES
Potted fish and fish pastes are very English. For centuries they were the delight of the well-to-do, especially the coveted lampreys of Gloucester and the char of Windermere. But potted fish of all sorts provided breakfasts for many a weary traveller, a canny way of preserving fish, and a convenient way of stretching small quantities. Once a thriving industry, only potted shrimps and pretty pot lids remain.

Most modern commercial fish pastes are by comparison cheap and nasty, with fish low on the list of ingredients. At home it can be a different matter. You need only fish, sweet unsalted butter and seasonings. The problem these days is the butter. Traditional recipes both ancient and modern call for equal proportions of butter and fish plus extra butter for sealing – a proportion I find unacceptably high and, given modern storage conditions, unnecessary. A proportion of 1:3 will give a very nice potted fish mixture. Smoked, oily fish such as kippers or mackerel can be successfully pounded together with one of the many low-fat, soft cheeses currently on the market. These, strictly speaking, do not deserve the name 'potted' or 'paste', but to call them pâté is gilding the lily. Think of them as a fish cream, if you prefer.

Potted Salmon, Trout, Crab, etc.

Weigh left-over cooked fish, remove any skin and bones, and flake roughly. Melt a third of its weight in butter and mix into the fish. Season with mace, nutmeg, salt, pepper, cayenne as appropriate, plus a few drops of lemon juice or anchovy essence for shellfish, if this appeals. Pack into little pots or ramekin dishes, making sure there are no air pockets, and chill until required. Decorate with a tiny sprig of parsley and serve with hot, dry toast or sliced brown bread as appropriate. To keep for a few days, cover when cold with a layer of clarified butter. Remove the butter before serving and use it for cooking.

If you have no cooked fish to hand and must start from scratch, cook the fish first in a moderate oven with seasonings and shavings of butter, covered with foil. Allow to cool and drain off all the juices – it is these which, if incorporated into the mixture, will sour the paste. Skin and pot in the usual way. For a fish paste, blend the fish and the melted butter until smooth and pack in pots as before. Smoked fish such as haddock should be covered first with boiling water. Let it stand for 10 minutes and then proceed in the usual manner.

This is the basic formula, but other potted fish dishes, using different herbs and spices, are equally successful. Gail Duff, for example, in her *Pick of the Crop*, suggests a mixture of cooked haddock, tarragon and redcurrants, which is original and good.

Smoked Fish Creams

Skin and bone smoked mackerel or cooked kipper fillets or smoked trout and blend or mash with a $\frac{1}{3}-\frac{1}{2}$ their weight of *quark*, Shape, other low fat cream cheese or thick, drained yoghurt. Add seasonings to taste, but this time choose differently – orange juice and a little orange rind, or the juice from a Seville orange, a pinch of curry powder, or herbs such as dill and chervil. Sharpen with lemon juice if necessary and pot in the usual way. Use fresh and accompany with thinly sliced brown bread.

COD A L'INDIENNE

4 cod steaks; 2 tablespoons mild curry powder mixed with 1 tablespoon flour, plus an extra tablespoon curry powder for cooking the pasta; 1½ lb / 675 g fresh tomatoes; 1 lb / 450 g tagliatelle or wholewheat semolina pasta; vegetable oil and butter for frying.

Wipe the fish and dip each piece into the curry and flour mixture making sure there's a good thick coating on each. Pour in enough oil to cover the base of a frying pan and when it's hot add the fish. Cook steadily for about 12–15 minutes, turning once until the fish is evenly browned and cooked through. Remove, and keep warm in a wide, shallow serving dish.

Meanwhile melt a knob of butter in another pan, add the tomatoes skinned and roughly chopped and let them cook gently for 5–10 minutes until they've melted sufficiently to produce their own sauce. Part of the charm of this dish lies in the freshness of the sauce, so resist the urge to boil madly or to cook longer. Check the seasoning, adding a pinch of sugar or dash of basil vinegar if this seems a good idea. Time the pasta to be ready at the same time as the fish and sauce, adding a tablespoon of curry powder to the cooking water. Spoon the sauce around the fish and serve the pasta separately.

CRAB OR SALMON QUENELLES

Until recently *quenelles* were not the sort of dish lightly tackled at home, requiring at least an afternoon's work to pound the fish into necessary smoothness. Now a food processor accomplishes this feat in a matter of moments. All the work can be done in advance, leaving you only to poach the dumplings (for that is all they are) and finish the sauce. Crab and salmon *quenelles* are prepared in exactly the same way. The seasonings should not be as robust for salmon as for crab.

These *quenelles* are far lower in calories than those made from more classic recipes. I find them equally delicious, and with the same melting delicate softness which is their characteristic. See what you think. This quantity will serve four as a first course or two as a main dish.

6 oz / 170 g fresh crab meat; 2 oz / 60 g white fish (plaice, lemon sole or whiting), free from skin and bone; 1 egg, 1 egg white; 2½ fl oz / 75 ml double cream.

For the sauce: shell and debris from the crab; 1 medium onion, sliced; stick of celery, chopped; 2 tomatoes, chopped; large glass of white wine; *bouquet garni* to include a little tarragon and fennel if possible; butter.

To finish: 1 large egg yolk plus 1 scant teaspoon potato flour slaked in milk; 1–2 tablespoons double cream; little brown crab meat; chopped chives or fennel.

Put both sorts of fish in a food processor, keeping back a dessertspoon or so of the brown crab meat to enrich the sauce, and process until smooth. Add the egg, egg white and cream and process again till the mixture resembles a thick, pinkish whipped cream. Transfer to a bowl, season to taste, cover, and chill in the refrigerator until required. Next make the stock for the sauce. Scrub the crab bones, legs and shell and sweat with the vegetables in a knob of butter, over a low heat for about 10 minutes, keeping them covered. Add the wine, seasonings and enough water to cover. Bring to the boil, skim, and simmer for 30–40 minutes. Strain and return to the rinsed out pan and then reduce to 8 fl oz / scant 250 ml, skimming as necessary. It should now be of a fine flavour. Set aside until needed.

For the final cooking and assembly of the dish, have a large pan full of lightly salted water, barely simmering. The success of your *quenelles* depends on this, for if the water more than murmurs, the *quenelles* may break up. I find it simplest to slip the *quenelles* into the water and then turn the heat off. Have a lightly buttered serving dish ready in a warm oven, the egg yolk beaten with the potato flour and a little stock at the ready, and the crab stock heating in a separate pan. Shape the *quenelles*, one at a time, between two medium sized spoons. At home I use some deep oval dessert spoons which give me nine *quenelles* from this mixture. As each one is formed, lower it gently into the simmering pan of water. Within seconds it should slip off the spoon easily. If not, ease it off gently. It will sink to the bottom only to rise again almost immediately. Poach gently for 5–7 minutes. Try the ninth – cook's perk – to check. It should still be slightly creamy inside.

Meanwhile finish the sauce. Pour the hot stock on to the egg mixture, whisking as you do so. Return to the pan and cook gently, stirring all the time until the sauce thickens somewhat. Don't allow the sauce to boil, though you can bring it safely to boiling point. Finish with cream and the reserved crab meat making any final adjustments to consistency and seasoning, adding a little cayenne, tomato purée or salt or pepper if it seems appropriate. Lift the *quenelles* out of their water-bath with a slotted spoon and drain briefly on a kitchen towel. Arrange in a warmed serving dish or on individual serving plates, spoon the sauce over, finish with a dusting of herbs and serve immediately. Plain rice and a crisp white wine to accompany. A fine dish.

MARINATED HALIBUT
WITH SORREL AND CREAM

I am indebted for this recipe to Geraldine Holt who devised it as a way of keeping fish for one or two days when time or circumstances do not allow for it to be cooked straightaway.

4 halibut steaks; 5 fl oz / 150 ml white wine; 1 clove garlic, sliced; handful of sorrel leaves, shredded; up to 1 oz / 30 g butter; 4 tablespoons double [or single cream]; salt and pepper (optional).

Place the fish steaks in a flat dish, pour over the wine and distribute the garlic amongst the fish making sure it's immersed in the wine. Cover and refrigerate for 24–48 hours, turning once. Lift out the fish, drain well and pat dry with kitchen paper. Melt ½ oz / 15 g butter in a pan, and when it's hot quickly seize the fish for a minute on each side. Remove and transfer to a heated ovenproof dish. Pour the marinade into the pan, bubble up for a minute or two and strain through a sieve over the fish. Cover the dish with buttered paper and cook in a moderate oven 180°C / 350°F / gas mark 4 for 10–15 minutes or until the fish is cooked. Transfer to a serving dish and keep warm. Melt another knob of butter in a small pan, add the sorrel and stir until softened. Pour in the cooking juices, reduce until it's slightly thickened, add the cream, heat through and spoon over the fish. Serve immediately with rice or a few plainly cooked potatoes to accompany.

PRAWNS IN OIL AND GARLIC

A sublime dish and worth saving up for.

Per person: 2 or 3 giant Mediterranean type prawns; 2 or 3 fat, juicy cloves of garlic; 1–2 dried chillies; olive oil for frying.

First prepare the prawns. Using a pair of scissors, cut away the legs and the under belly part of the shell. Gently ease the prawn out of its shell, run a sharp knife along the centre of its back just deep enough to expose the long, thin alimentary canal, and remove this with the point of your knife. Replace the prawn in its shell. (None of this is strictly necessary, but it so improves the enjoyment of eating the prawns it's more than worth the small amount of effort involved.) If the garlic is less than fresh, or is likely to affect your digestion adversely, blanch it first for a minute in boiling water, drain and dry.

To cook the prawns, pour in enough fruity olive oil to generously cover the base of a frying pan or sauté dish which will just hold the prawns comfortably. Add the chillies and the garlic and gently cook for a couple of minutes, time enough for the chillies to give bite to the oil and for the garlic to soften somewhat. Add the prawns and continue cooking until the shells are crisp and the flesh white. Serve immediately with pitta bread and eat out of the same pan, with your fingers. If you have small gratin dishes each portion can be cooked individually. An acceptable second best are prawns which have been previously boiled. Adjust the cooking times accordingly and cook them briefly; 2–3 minutes should be enough.

Do not attempt to eat the dried chillies and advise others likewise.

SALMON AND CUCUMBER KEBABS

A recipe from American cooks Paula Peck and Julia Child for stretching salmon, using up odd portions, or for the imported kind.

Marinate diced 1 in / 2.5 cm cubes of salmon and peeled cucumber in a mixture of 1 part soy sauce: 4 parts white wine, plus a good pinch of sugar, for 1–2 hours. Five tablespoons of marinade should be enough for 8 oz / 225 g of each. Thread on to wooden skewers, brush with a little melted butter and grill – if it's over charcoal so much the better – for 7–8 minutes, turning occasionally. If using an electric or gas grill, baste with some of the marinade. Serve either as a first course on a bed of shredded lettuce leaves, or as a main course with rice. Mustard and dill sauce makes a good accompaniment.

THE CAPTAIN'S SCALLOPS

The best scallops I have ever eaten were bought on holiday in Salcombe, Devon. Large, translucent and mouth-wateringly juicy, a taste of the sea I shall remember for a good while yet. At home it's a different matter. Living as I do at the other end of the country, such scallops as I can find cannot hope to compare. For them, something a little adventurous is required. The result – one of the best recipes in this book.

2–3 scallops per person; $\frac{1}{2}$ in / 1$\frac{1}{4}$ cm slice of fresh ginger, peeled and cut into the finest *julienne* shreds; 4–5 fl oz / 120–150 ml single cream; ½ teaspoon mild curry powder; 2–3 tablespoons dry white wine.

Clean the scallops and remove the membrane which surrounds their girth but leave the coral attached. Sprinkle the shredded ginger on to the base of a shallow dish – a soup plate is ideal – and place the scallops on top in a single layer. Moisten with the wine, cover with a plate or lid and cook over a pan of gently boiling water for 3–5 minutes or until the scallops have turned opaque and are just cooked. Remove and keep warm. Transfer the cooking liquor to a pan, keeping back the shredded ginger for decoration, and boil down to 4–5 tablespoons.

In the meantime start the sauce. Simmer the cream and curry powder very gently in a small heavy pan until it has reduced by at least a half, stirring often with a small whisk. It will thicken considerably. Add the cooking juices gradually whisking vigorously. The sauce will become light and foamy. Arrange the scallops on hot serving plates, spoon over a little of the sauce, decorate each with a pinch of ginger shreds and serve immediately as a first course.

BELL INN SMOKIES
This is one of my favourite dishes from the *Observer*'s 'British Cookery' series of 1984. Arbroath smokies are one delicacy which seems to have a better distribution than some.

For each person you need a small ramekin dish, some skinned, seeded and chopped ripe tomato, some flaked Arbroath smokie (i.e. small, whole, undyed smoked haddock), skin and bones removed, and a little cream. At the Bell Inn near Aylesbury, source of the recipe, they use double cream but single will suffice.

Cover the base of each ramekin with a layer of tomato, add a thicker layer of fish almost to the rim, and top with cream. Either slip under a pre-heated grill which is simpler and works very well, or cook at the top of a hot oven until the mixture is lightly browned and bubbling. Serve on small plates with triangles of hot dry toast. A little finely chopped tarragon or fennel mixed in with the tomato makes a pleasant addition.

SENHORINA PAIXAO'S LULA (STUFFED SQUID)
1 medium squid per person; 2 onions; 1 green pepper, sliced and seeds removed; 2–3 chopped cloves of garlic; pinch of piri piri (dried chilli flakes or use 1 dried chilli); 2 lb / 900 g tomatoes; 4–6 oz / 120–170 g mild gammon or lean bacon in a piece; 2–3 tablespoons olive oil; 2–3

allspice berries; 1 tablespoon chopped parsley; large glass of white wine.

Dice the bacon into small pieces and chop all the other vegetables finely. Clean the squid, remove the tentacles, chop these and mix with the vegetables, bacon and parsley. Stuff the squid with some of the mixture and loosely close the ends with a toothpick so that the stuffing doesn't fall out during cooking. Put the rest of the mixture into a fairly deep pan, add the seasonings, olive oil and wine and place the squid on top. Cover and cook gently for about 45 minutes or until the squid are tender and the sauce thick. If at the end of the cooking time the sauce is still watery, remove the squid and reduce it further.

Serve the squid in its sauce accompanied by plain rice, preferably the round grain sort they use in Portugal.

TROUT NACH STARNBERGER ART

Clean and dry your trout, sprinkle the insides with Worcester or soy sauce and set aside in the refrigerator until needed. For 2 trout chop together a small bunch of parsley leaves with a sprig of tarragon, a shallot or piece of onion and 1–2 teaspoons of capers until all are reduced to a dark green pulp. Heat enough vegetable oil to cover the base of a frying pan, adding, if you like, a rasher of streaky bacon to flavour the oil. Lightly dust the fish with flour, shake off all the excess and fry over a moderate heat for 4–5 minutes each side or until the trout are cooked and the skins nicely browned. Remove to a serving dish and keep warm, uncovered, in a warm oven. Drain off any remaining oil and remove the bacon. Add $\frac{1}{2}$ oz / 15 g of butter and soften the herb paste in this for a minute or so. Stir in the juice of half a lemon, cook a little longer, 2–3 minutes, and soften with a little single cream. Spoon over the trout and serve immediately, garnished with wedges of lemon or sweet orange and a few plainly cooked potatoes to accompany.

I cannot contemplate frying more than two trout at a time. For larger numbers, grilling seems more satisfactory. It's also lighter. Score the flesh with a couple of diagonal cuts, sprinkle the cavities with soy sauce or Worcester as before, paint the skin with oil and grill for approximately 5 minutes each side. Make the sauce separately, adjusting all the quantities except the butter – you need only sufficient to cover the pan. Spoon the sauce over the trout and serve.

POACHED FISH IN NUT SAUCE

A fine fish dish from Spain, suitable for any kind of white fish. The sauce comes out lime green, speckled with orange coloured flecks of saffron. Unexpected and most attractive.

4 thick fish fillets; water for poaching plus 2–3 bay leaves.

For the sauce: 2 oz / 60 g blanched almonds or a mixture of blanched almonds and hazelnuts; 2 tablespoons chopped parsley; generous pinch of saffron; large clove of garlic, crushed; ½ slice dry, toasted white bread.

Blend all the sauce ingredients to a smooth paste in a blender or food processor and transfer to a small pan. Pour enough water into a shallow pan to cover the fish, salt lightly, add the bay leaves and bring to simmering point. Immerse the fish and poach gently until *just* cooked. Take out the fish, drain, remove any skin and arrange neatly in a warmed serving dish. Put into a warm oven, loosely covered with foil, while you finish the sauce. Add enough of the poaching liquid to the paste to make a light creamy sauce of medium consistency. Bring to the boil, cook for just one minute and pour over the fish fillets. Serve with rice and a plain green salad to which a few strips of red pepper have been added.

FISH FILLETS WITH SPRING ONION AND GINGER

A recipe in the Chinese style, but with European touches. Excellent for any of the finer, more delicate fish fillets such as plaice, lemon sole or halibut. Choose large fillets if you can, allowing half per person.

2 large or 4 medium fish fillets; approx. 5 fl oz / 150 ml dry white wine; ½ in / 1.25 cm stick of fresh ginger, peeled and cut into tiny *julienne* strips; 3–4 spring onions, shredded into thin strips 2–3 in / 5–7.5 cm long; 2–3 tablespoons single cream, or creamy milk.

Butter a large, shallow dish and lay the fillets, skin side down, overlapping them slightly if necessary. Pour over the wine and scatter the *julienne* of ginger round the sides so that they lie in the liquid. Leave for an hour or so in a cool place. When the time comes to cook the fish, distribute the spring onions over the top, baste with the wine, and cover loosely with foil. Bake in a moderately hot oven, 190°C / 375°F / gas mark 5, for 20–25 minutes or until just cooked. Remove from the oven and transfer the dish to the top of the stove. Add enough cream to soften the cooking juices, stir to amalgamate, bring to the boil and check the taste. Spoon the juices over the fish and serve from the same pan, with rice or plain potatoes.

GNOCCHI DI PESCE

8 oz / 225 g filleted plaice or whiting, skin and bones removed (allow a generous 10 oz / 300 g bought weight); 4 oz / 120 g ricotta or cottage cheese; 1 large egg white; 4 fl oz / 120 ml single cream.

For the sauce: 4 tablespoons fish *fumet* (concentrated fish stock); 2 tablespoons dry white wine; 1 large egg yolk; 2 tablespoons single cream; 2 tomatoes skinned, seeded and sliced into segments; finely chopped fennel.

Reduce the first 4 ingredients to a smooth cream in a food processor or blender. Transfer to a bowl, cover, and chill until required. Just before you come to cook the *gnocchi*, assemble the sauce ingredients. Have 4 small plates warming in the oven and a large pan of lightly salted water to hand. Put the tomato segments to warm, reserving their juice and pulp. Shape the fish mixture into 4 large *quenelles* (see p. 122), using 2 large, deep, oval serving spoons. You will easily get 4 out of this mixture and may get one or two more depending on the size of your spoon. Slip each one into the barely simmering water and poach for 7–8 minutes.

Meanwhile make the sauce. Whisk the first 3 ingredients in a bowl over a pan of hot water until light and foamy. Stir in the cream, a little of the sieved, reserved tomato pulp and a very little finely chopped fennel, adding these last two to taste. The whole operation shouldn't take more than 5 minutes, and the *gnocchi* can be left in their poaching water for up to 5 minutes without coming to any harm, so getting everything right at the same time shouldn't present any difficulties. In fact, this is a remarkably easy recipe and looks far more impressive than the actual work involved merits.

Divide the sauce between the plates, sit one of the snow-white *gnocchi* on top, garnish with a tiny frond of fennel spreadeagled across its back, and arrange a couple of warmed tomato segments either side. Serve immediately as a first course, with a fresh tomato *coulis* if preferred to the above sauce.

FISH STEAKS BAKED IN LEMON CREAM

A simple, mildly refreshing dish, for white fish of quality.

4 thick fish steaks; 4 fl oz / 120 ml yoghurt; 4 fl oz / 120 ml single cream; 1 tablespoon finely grated onion; finely grated rind and juice of 1 lemon.

For decoration: thinly cut slices of lemon; finely chopped dill or chives.

Wipe the fish and lay, side-by-side, in a buttered ovenproof dish. Drain the yoghurt until it is almost solid and mix with the other ingredients to form a smooth cream. The mixture should be very thick, so add lemon juice accordingly. Carefully spoon the topping over the surface of the steaks and leave for a couple of hours in the refrigerator, or longer if it suits, covered with cling film. Bake in a preheated oven 180°C / 350°F / gas mark 4 for about 25–30 minutes. The topping will set to a creamy curd and there will be just a little clear juice surrounding the fish. Decorate with a line of dill or chives down the centre and surround with the thinnest slices of lemon. Serve with a saffron rice (made by adding a good pinch of powdered saffron and a glass of wine when cooking), to which a few plump black raisins have been added.

FISH PILAFF
For 3–4 servings:
1 lb / 450 g firm white fish, skinned, bones removed and cut into large chunks; 8 oz / 225 g basmati rice; 1 onion, finely chopped; 1 tablespoon vegetable oil; good pinch of powdered saffron; ½ teaspoon ground cumin plus 1 teaspoon whole cumin seeds; 2–3 cloves; bay leaf; 10 fl oz / 300 ml water; salt.

To finish: 2 tablespoons raisins; 2 oz / 60 g dried apricots; 2 tablespoons pine kernels; finely chopped coriander; few prawns (optional); knob of butter.

Cover the apricots with boiling water and set aside to plump up. Heat the oil in a heavy casserole and gently soften the onions. Stir in the cumin, fry for a minute and then add the rice and saffron powdered in the usual way (see p. 76). If you have no saffron, use ½ teaspoon of turmeric; it is not a substitute, and the flavour of the dish will change slightly, but the colour will be approximately the same. Keep stirring until the rice is translucent. Distribute the fish over the top, add the rest of the seasonings, a pinch of salt and the liquid, using the soaking liquor plus extra water to make up to ½ pint / 300 ml. Bring to the boil, cover and cook over the lowest heat until the liquid has evaporated.

Meanwhile, gently fry the drained apricots, cut into neat slivers, with the raisins and pine kernels in a small pan until the raisins have plumped and the pine kernels are lightly browned. Once the water has been absorbed, gently mix the fruit into the pilaff, at the same time breaking up the fish into smaller pieces. Replace the lid, turn off the heat and leave to stand for 10 minutes, during which time the rice and fish will finish cooking. Finish with chopped coriander and a few pink prawns and serve immediately with a green or tomato salad.

FISH STEW IN THE PROVENÇAL STYLE

1½–2 lb / 675–900 g firm fleshed fish; 30 fl oz / 850 ml fish stock made from the trimmings and a few prawn shells if possible; 6–8 oz / 170–225 g each finely sliced onion and white part of leek; 8 fl oz / 225 ml fresh tomato sauce or equivalent quantity of sieved canned tomatoes; large glass of dry white wine; ¼ teaspoon fennel seeds; small piece of dried orange peel; *bouquet garni* to include thyme, parsley and if possible fennel; 2 tablespoons olive oil; a few stoned and halved black olives; garlic croûtes; few mussels (optional); 4–6 cloves of garlic, crushed.

You can use any sort of firm fleshed fish for this dish, but not the oily kind. A selection is preferable, and those who have access to a wider variety than I, will find the stew improved by it. Choose thick fillets and cut them into neat sizeable chunks. I prefer to skin mine and remove any obvious bones.

Begin by sweating the onions, leeks and garlic in a largish pan until soft and beginning to give up their juices. Do this slowly and carefully and keep them covered, they shouldn't brown but merely colour slightly. Add the wine, followed by the tomatoes, stock and seasonings and cook steadily until the sauce is thick, a good 45 minutes or so – this point is important. The juices from the fish will dilute the sauce considerably, so allow for this in your initial reduction. Remove the herbs and orange rind and transfer the sauce to a wide shallow pan. Lay the fish on top, baste with the sauce, scatter over the olives and cook very gently until the fish is done, basting occasionally and turning the pieces over half way through if need be. At this stage add the mussels and their liquor, previously opened in the usual way. Sprinkle with parsley, tuck garlic croûtes around the edge, serve with pasta and dream of holidays in the sun.

FISH THE PORTUGUESE WAY

On holiday in Portugal, two dishes especially caught my imagination: *caldeirada*, a fish and potato stew, and *lula*, stuffed squid (see p. 126).

Caldeirada

There is no one recipe for this dish. Within a basic framework of fish, potato and tomatoes, *caldeirada* is whatever the cook wants it to be. What makes it so good is that the fish is always fresh – landed that morning or minutes before. This version is the one we ate in a beach café at Sagres, the southernmost tip of the Algarve. It contained no more than potatoes, sardines, dog fish and a little striped fish I never did find the name for, bathed in a thinnish red sauce of incomparable flavour, and topped with a few slices of tomato. We both agreed it was one of the best meals we ate during our stay. It would be foolish optimism to think it could ever taste the same as it did then – recipes may travel, but ingredients, formica topped tables, and the smell of the sea do not. Yet the idea was so simple and so good it was worth recording. This is the nearest approximation I can get to that particular *caldeirada* but don't be afraid to work on it; peppers, onions and seasonings such as coriander, bay leaves, parsley and garlic are all frequent additions, and fish stock, if available, can be used instead of plain water.

Peel or scrape and cut up into largish slices as many potatoes of the waxy kind as you think right for the number of people eating and put them into a pan with 2–3 tablespoons of fruity olive oil, a good teaspoon of paprika, fresh or dried oregano and 1 or 2 dried chillies. Add a glass of wine and enough water just to cover, put the lid on and boil hard until the potatoes are half cooked. Now add a selection of prepared fish, at least 2 or 3 sorts. In the absence of anything interesting, a few shellfish added towards the end of cooking are a good idea, otherwise try and vary white fish with something like gurnard or grey or red mullet, or squid or conger eel if you have the taste for it. Small fish can be left whole, larger fish should be cut into steaks or large pieces as appropriate. Cover with sliced tomatoes and cook more gently until the fish is ready, adding a little more water if necessary. The sauce should have bite but not be too hot, so remove the chillies when the flavour seems right. Check the seasoning. Serve from the same pan with bread.

Rice, Pasta, Grains & Pulses

There was an Old Person of Dean,
Who dined on one Pea and one Bean;
For he said, 'More than that
Would make me too fat,'
That cautious Old Person of Dean.

EDWARD LEAR *Edward Lear's Nonsense Omnibus*, 1943

These are our primitive foods, with much to offer. Pasta is convenient and responds to simple sauces, many of which can be quickly made with a few store cupboard items and maybe a tomato or two. It is equally delicious dressed simply with olive oil. For tired and hungry people nothing could be finer. Rice is more versatile. Its great dishes are its pilaffs and risottos, of which there are endless variations using meat, fish, vegetables and fruit. It makes excellent salads and stuffings. Plain hot rice is lovely. Infused with herbs or spices, or with coconut milk or wine, it makes a welcome addition to diets based on bread and potatoes. Grains are for warming winter dishes. They combine well with vegetables in casseroles and they too make excellent pilaffs. Dried beans and pulses add valuable proteins. Sprouted, they take on new life and exciting possibilities. These are foods whose time has come.

We have certainly travelled a long way from the day my grandmother opened her first tin of spaghetti. 'Worms', she gasped, and threw them to the chickens. Sixty years on, kitchen shops do a brisk business in pasta machines, and jars of beans sprout merrily in suburban kitchens.

Rice   *To Boil Rice for Curry; the recipe of a native Indian cook.*
'Wash him well; much wash in cold water; rice flour make him stick; water boil already very fast. Shove him in; rice not burn, water shake him too much. Boil twenty minutes. Rub one rice in thumb and finger; if it all rub away, him quite done. Put rice in colander. Hot water run away through; put cold water through him; then put back in pan, cover him and keep hot; then rice soon all ready. Eat him up!'
ERROLL SHERSON *The Book of Vegetable Cookery,* 1931

Plain, boiled white rice
My own method of cooking rice. It produces a rice of good flavour, with more bite than usual and nicely dry. It is important to choose a heavy pan which will retain its heat.

Wash the rice in several changes of cold water until the water is more or less clear. Cover with fresh water and leave to soak for at least half an hour. When the time comes to cook the rice, rinse it once more and add enough fresh water to come level with the rice. Measured, this quantity approximates to the same weight of dry rice. For 8 oz / 225 g rice you need about 8 fl oz / 225 ml of water. Add a good pinch of salt, bring to the boil, cover and boil hard for one minute. Remove from the heat. Let the rice stand for 10–15 minutes. It will continue to cook in its own steam and can happily wait for up to half an hour in total. Fluff lightly with a fork and serve. Alternatively, transfer to a warm, lightly buttered dish and keep hot until required.

Brown rice
a. Cover the rice with enough water to come *above* the level of the rice by an inch or so. Bring to the boil and boil hard for 5 minutes. Drain, add fresh water just to cover and a pinch of salt and bring to the boil. Cover and cook over a very low heat until all the water has been absorbed. Depending on your rice, this will take about 15–20 minutes. Turn off the heat and allow the rice to stand for a further 5–10 minutes. It should be soft, chewy and dry. If the rice isn't quite cooked, add a couple of tablespoons of water and continue cooking over a low heat for a few minutes more.

b. Cover the rice with a lot of water, add a pinch of salt, bring to the boil, skim off any scum and boil hard for 5 minutes. Turn off the heat, cover and leave the rice undisturbed to cool in its liquid by which time most of the grains will have burst and the rice will be all but cooked. Pour off most of the water and reheat gently to complete the cooking.

This is a useful method of preparing brown rice in advance, or for cold dishes. It produces a slightly softer result than the first method.

PERSIAN HERBED RICE

A dish I first came across in Claudia Roden's *A Book of Middle Eastern Food*. Good in summer to accompany charcoal grilled kebabs or fish, or with veal and chicken dishes. Pick a good handful of fresh herbs – tarragon, chives, parsley, coriander, oregano or dill – and wash and chop finely. About 5 or 10 minutes before you serve the rice, scatter the herbs over the top. Just before serving, lightly fork them in. The rice will be beautifully fragrant and speckled with green.

COCONUT RICE

A South East Asian way of cooking rice, a change from the usual spiced rice, delicate and not too strongly flavoured with coconut. The obvious accompaniments are Thai-style dishes, but it could also be served with plainly grilled pork chops or chicken. Try it also as a base for a prawn pilaff. Fresh coconut will produce a better and slightly sweeter flavour but I don't think that for this dish it's worth going to the extra trouble unless you have some in the freezer.

12 oz / 340 g rice, basmati for preference; approx. 12 fl oz / 340 ml water; 4 oz / 120 g finely grated fresh coconut, or 2 oz / 60 g desiccated coconut; pinch of salt; 1 in / 2.5 cm stick of cinnamon; lightly toasted coconut flakes (optional).

Pour boiling water over the coconut and leave to infuse for 30 minutes or so. Strain, saving the milky fluid and pressing hard to extract from the coconut as much of the juice as possible. If you can be bothered, repeat the process a second time. But be careful not to use more than the total amount of liquid needed to cook the rice. Make up to 12 fl oz/340 ml with the rest of the water. Meanwhile, wash and soak the rice in the usual way. Cook the rice as described for plain boiled rice, using the coconut liquid and adding the stick of cinnamon. Fluff up and either decorate with toasted coconut flakes or serve these separately in a small bowl. They're not strictly necessary but provide a nice crunchy contrast.

PERFUMED BASMATI RICE

An exquisitely fragrant rice, adapted from *Madhur Jaffrey's Indian Cookery*. I have reduced the butter and salt, and shortened the cooking time.

12 oz / 340 Basmati rice; approx. 12 fl oz / 340 ml water; ¾ teaspoon ground turmeric; 3–4 cloves; 1 in / 2.5 cm stick of cinnamon; 3 bay leaves; pinch of salt; ⅓–½ oz / 10–15 g butter or ghee.

Prepare and cook the rice as described for plain boiled rice, adding all the seasonings with the water. Just before serving, dot the surface with tiny dabs of butter or ghee and mix them lightly into the rice with a fork. Serve with Indian dishes or plain grilled chicken or lamb.

POLYNESIAN RICE

A romantic name and a sweetish dish, incorporating fresh fruit and brown rice, which is high in goodness as well as flavour. I find it irresistible. Serve as a main dish with yoghurt and salads or with Chinese-style food. This amount serves 3–4.

12 oz / 340 g brown rice, parboiled for 5 minutes and drained; small onion, finely chopped; 8 fl oz / 225 ml fresh pineapple or orange juice; 2–3 oz / 60–90 g chopped walnuts; 1 large sliced banana; 1 orange, divided into segments with the skin and pith removed; 2–3 slices of fresh pineapple cut into chunks; 1 tablespoon vegetable oil.

In a heavy pan gently sweat the onion in the oil until soft. Add the rice and the fruit juice and enough water to bring the liquid up to the level of the rice. Cover and cook gently until all the liquid has been absorbed and the rice is cooked. Stir in the chopped walnuts and the fruit – you don't have to use all three. Replace the lid and let the mixture stand for 5–10 minutes to allow the flavours to develop and the fruit to heat through. Serve in the same dish, with a bowl of plain yoghurt.

UN-FRIED STIR-FRIED RICE

A useful and adaptable dish. Ingredients and seasonings can be varied to suit.

12 oz / 340 g cooked hot rice; 4 oz / 120 g cooked peas; 4–6 oz / 120–170 g shelled prawns; small onion / spring onions / leek, finely sliced; ½ diced red or green pepper; strips of Chinese omelette (see method); 1–2 tablespoons vegetable oil; soy sauce (optional); 4/5 teaspoons sherry.

First make the omelettes. Beat together 2 eggs and make 4 or 5 thin omelettes using just enough mixture to coat the base of a lightly greased omelette pan. When one side is cooked, turn the omelette over and cook the other side for about a minute. Lift one edge of the omelette and pour in a teaspoon of sherry – it will sizzle violently. Remove, set aside and repeat the process until all the egg mixture is used up. When all the omelettes have been cooked, roll them together, cut into thin shreds and keep warm.

To finish the rice, soften whichever onion you're using in a tablespoon of oil in a smallish pan. Add any other uncooked vegetables and continue cooking over a low heat until these, too, are just cooked. Add the peas, followed by the prawns. Cook until the prawns have heated through and spoon the mixture over the top of the rice. Decorate with the omelette strips, sprinkle with a little soy sauce and serve immediately in the pan in which the rice was cooked.

Other rice recipes: see spiced chicken or lamb pilaff p. 104, and fish pilaff p. 130.

HOMEMADE PASTA
Making pasta is a pleasurable thing to do. The process is simple: you take eggs, flour, and a little salt, mix them together to form a dough, roll the dough out thinly, and cut it how you want. However, a few details will help.

Use strong bread flour and fresh eggs and let the dough rest before rolling it out. This gives the gluten in the flour time to relax. One large egg will incorporate up to 4 oz / 120 g of flour. This makes enough pasta for 4 small first-course servings. For a main course allow 4 oz / 120 g of pasta per person. If you are serving a substantial meat or fish dish, 2–3 oz / 60–90 g should suffice. Olive oil is an optional extra which can be incorporated into the dough but only sparingly.

Once the pasta has been rolled out, let it dry a little before cutting. This helps to prevent the pieces from sticking together which can be a problem when it is very fresh. You don't want to dry the pasta so much that it becomes too brittle to cut successfully; up to an hour is usually about right.

To cook the pasta, use your biggest pan, full of briskly boiling water. I allow up to a tablespoon of salt per large potful. A little olive oil can also be added. Feed the pasta into the water and give it a good stir around. Fresh pasta takes anything from 30 seconds to 4–5 minutes to cook, depending on how long you've let it dry out, and how thick or thin it is.

Dried, pasta will easily keep one or two weeks in the refrigerator, and freezes well in its uncooked state.

Making pasta by hand
2 eggs; approx. 8 oz / 225 g flour; ½ teaspoon salt; 1 tablespoon olive oil (optional).

Sift the flour and salt on to a work surface, make a well in the centre and break in the eggs. Add the olive oil if you're using it. Using your fingers, gradually work the flour into the eggs, drawing the flour in from the sides as you go along, a messy but pleasant enough job. When all the flour has been incorporated, knead until the dough is smooth and pliable. Cover with cling film and let it rest, preferably for an hour or so. If you're short of time you can give it less. Cut off a portion of the dough, place it on a large floured surface and start to roll it out. Start by rolling the dough as if you were rolling shortcrust pastry. When it gets quite thin, tease and stretch it out with your fingers. Finish rolling with short, sharp movements, working on one part of the dough at a time. This sounds more complicated than it actually is. It is quicker than trying to roll the ever increasing sheet of dough evenly. As soon as the dough is as thin as you want, hang it over a kitchen chair and repeat the process with the rest. Keep your rolling pin and work surface well floured throughout; the dough should emerge smooth and silky.

Cut the pasta whilst it is still pliable as required. For ravioli, use a pastry cutter, for everything else a sharp knife. Tagliatelle is commonly made by rolling the dough up like a swiss roll and then cutting across to form thin ribbons, but it's just to quick to run the knife along the length of the dough and it saves having to undo the curls. Spread the pasta out on to a clean cloth or, again, over a kitchen chair, keeping the strands as separate as you can.

Making pasta using a food processor
Making pasta by hand is both fun and instructive but does undeniably take time. A food processor gives good results in a fraction of the time and with a lot less effort. The method I generally follow is the one that appeared in a *Sunday Times* cookery course in 1984. This incorporates extra egg white into the standard mix which means that for every egg used, you get half as much again of pasta. But use a standard recipe if you wish; the method remains the same.

1 egg + 1 egg white; approx. 6 oz /170 g flour; ¼–½ teaspoon salt; 1 dessertspoon olive oil.

Put the egg, egg white, olive oil and salt in the food processor and process for 30 seconds. Add the flour and process for another 30 seconds or so, until the flour and egg mixture forms into a ball of dough. Don't process beyond this point. Scrape out the dough on to a floured surface and knead briefly until smooth, adding a little more flour if necessary. Cover with cling film and proceed as in the previous recipe. This makes enough pasta to serve two comfortably. For four servings, repeat the process making another batch of dough in the same way.

THREE PASTAS

Wholemeal Semolina Pasta
An outright winner. A nutritious pasta, with a mild, nutty flavour and one which combines the appeal of white pasta with the nutritional value of brown. The pasta I make most of the time.

2 eggs; 4 oz / 120 g strong white flour; 4 oz / 120 g wholewheat semolina (available from wholefood stores); ½ teaspoon salt; 1 tablespoon olive oil (optional).

Make the pasta in the usual way, either by hand or in a food processor. It makes a stiffer dough than normal pasta and, like wholemeal bread, is a bit more difficult to knead, but otherwise it handles exactly the same. Adding egg whites, as in the recipe above, also gives most satisfactory results. This quantity will serve 2–3 as a main course, but you may prefer to try it in half quantities initially to get the feel of it.

Fresh Herb Pasta
A lovely summertime pasta, best appreciated on its own. Tossed in a little butter, single cream or a sauce made by thinning down ricotta cheese with a little of the cooking water, this makes a delightful first course.

Add a couple of tablespoons of finely chopped herbs to your usual pasta dough, incorporating them with the eggs. You may need a little extra flour, depending on the moisture content of the herbs, but otherwise it handles the same as ordinary pasta dough. The choice of herbs is entirely up to you. Try to include a little tarragon.

Chocolate Pasta
A strange and bizarre pasta. The taste is not nearly as odd or as startling as you'd imagine. The colour – a deep, rich, chocolate brown – is magnificent. Try it on its own as a first course with the sauce below, or

with strong flavoured game such as pigeon or teal. Add ½–1 oz / 15–30 g cocoa, sifted with the flour, to your usual pasta dough, and proceed as before.

SAUCES FOR PASTA

There are many sauces which go well with pasta, most of which take little time and effort. Sauces based on tomatoes, mushrooms, ham, Italian cheeses, and savoury mixtures such as *pesto*, are obvious examples, but almost anything can be used to good effect. All the sauces and dishes that follow are equally suitable for fresh or dried pasta. Whether this is white or wholewheat is largely a matter of personal preference. One or two of the sauces and dishes are, I think, more appropriate to either one or the other, but most are suitable for both.

Pasta and Pesto

The sauce for pasta *par excellence*; summer would be unthinkable without it.

Large bunch of basil leaves, up to 2 oz / 60 g; 1 oz / 30 g pine kernels or walnuts; 1 oz / 30 g finely grated fresh Parmesan or Pecorino; 3–4 tablespoons of cold pressed olive oil, Tuscan for preference; 1 fat, juicy clove of garlic, crushed and chopped.

Begin by finely chopping each ingredient separately – this makes the work of pounding them together that much easier. Transfer the basil and the garlic to a mortar and pound to a thick, homogenous purée. Add the nuts, pound again, and then mix in the cheese. Gradually add enough olive oil to moisten the paste. The sauce should end up very thick, the consistency of softened butter.

Those of us who grow basil can afford the luxury of large handfuls for our *pesto*, but less will still produce a respectable sauce. Avoid packet Parmesan. Pecorino (originally the cheese of choice in Genoa, home of *pesto*) is far better, and is what I generally use myself. Walnuts give a different taste and are good for a change. Use the best you can find and remove the skins by pouring boiling water over them.

Pesto can be made very successfully in a food processor. Chop the basil and garlic as before and process with the nuts and cheese until you get a smooth paste, adding the olive oil cautiously at the end to get the desired consistency. Serve the *pesto* in a little bowl or earthenware pot for each person to help themselves, thinned down maybe with another few drops of olive oil. It will keep, under a protective layer of olive oil, in the refrigerator for up to a month. Don't confine *pesto* to pasta. It's almost as good with potatoes and summer vegetables, and will improve many a soup.

Summer Sauce

Drain about 8 fl oz / 250 ml of plain yoghurt until it is very thick. Beat in 2–4 tablespoons of single cream and a selection of fresh summer herbs, all chopped very finely. Toss the well-drained pasta in the sauce and serve immediately on very hot plates. Hand black pepper separately.

Agresto

A classic Italian sauce, rather sharp, which is served with roast beef or strong flavoured game as well as pasta.

2 oz / 60 g walnuts; 2 oz / 60 g almonds; 2 thin slices of white bread, crusts removed; tablespoon chopped parsley; juice of 1 lemon; rind of ½ lemon, finely grated; clove of garlic, chopped; ½ small onion, chopped (optional); approx. 4 fl oz / 120 ml tepid chicken stock; ½–1 teaspoon sugar; black pepper.

Remove the skins from the almonds and walnuts by soaking them briefly in boiling water. They should then peel off easily. A fiddly but essential job if the sauce is not to have that bitter tang that comes from unskinned nuts.

Blend the nuts, lemon juice and lemon rind briefly in a blender or food processor until they form a paste. Add the rest of the ingredients (except the stock and seasoning) and process again until everything is well mixed. Add enough tepid stock to give a thick sauce-like consistency and blend once more until smooth. Transfer to a pan, add a little freshly ground pepper and just enough sugar to bring out the flavour of the sauce without making it in any way sweet. Cook very gently over a low heat for two minutes without letting the sauce boil. It will thicken slightly and is now ready to use. Keep in the refrigerator, under a protective layer of oil.

To accompany meat, keep the sauce thick. For pasta, take as much sauce as you need to lubricate the pasta and dilute slightly with a little hot water. Toss the pasta in the sauce and serve immediately dusted with a little extra finely chopped parsley.

Avocado Sauce

Something of a cheat – but it does make an excellent and unusual sauce for pasta. Turn to p. 119 and the recipe for agates of avocado. Thin down the mixture with a little of the cooking water and lightly mix into the prepared pasta. The lime gives the sauce a refreshing sharpness. Adding a tablespoon of olive oil to the sauce mellows it, as does omitting the lime and adding a final sprinkling of chopped basil. Serve as a first course.

Lenten Sauce

A sauce adapted from *Syllabub in the Kitchen* by Philip Aiden. Chop together a large clove of garlic, a couple of tablespoons of parsley with a tablespoon each of mint, basil and watercress. Chop until everything is reduced almost to a purée. Melt about 2 oz / 60 g butter, stir in the herbs, and the sauce is ready. Toss the pasta in the sauce and serve immediately with grated Pecorino. An excellent and simply made sauce.

Ricotta and Brandy Sauce for Chocolate Pasta

This looks lovely, like chocolate ripple ice cream. Add the brandy cautiously – it gives a decided kick which is delicious, but which can easily become overpowering.

8 oz / 225 g sieved ricotta cheese; 1–2 tablespoons brandy; approx. 4 tablespoons creamy milk or single cream; 2 tablespoons toasted almond flakes or pine kernels.

Blend the ricotta cheese with the milk and brandy to form a smooth sauce with the consistency of double cream. Distribute the cooked pasta between 4 very hot plates, spoon the sauce over, scatter discreetly with the nuts and serve immediately as a first course.

Tomato and Apple Sauce

Heat a tablespoon of olive oil in a pan and add approximately equal quantities of peeled, chopped and not too tart cooking apples and skinned, fresh tomatoes, together with a stick of celery and a bay leaf. Unless your tomatoes are very good add a teaspoon of tomato purée as well. Cook until the apples and tomatoes are reduced to a thick pulp. Remove the celery and bay leaf, taste to check the seasoning, adding a pinch of sugar if necessary. Transfer to a serving boat and serve with plain pasta. Grated Parmesan or Pecorino can be handed separately, though I prefer it plain.

Tomato and Walnut Sauce

A good store cupboard sauce. Chop a good handful of walnuts very finely and gently fry them in 2 tablespoons of olive oil until they begin to go brown and crisp. Add 10 fl oz / 300 ml of tomato sauce and cook for about 5 minutes. The sauce will darken and thicken a little. Stir in some finely chopped basil and serve with plain pasta.

Uncooked Tomato Sauces

These make the freshest of all tomato sauces but they do need tomatoes of quality. Here are three variations – quantities are left to your discretion.

(a) Toss the cooked pasta in 1–2 tablespoons of fruity olive oil, stir in some skinned and chopped tomatoes, squeeze over the juice of one or more lemons, sprinkle with chopped basil and serve immediately on very hot plates.

(b) Blend together a small sweet red pepper with an equal quantity of skinned tomatoes drained of their juice. Add a little milk and Parmesan cheese to taste. Mix into the pasta and serve.

(c) Marinate chopped, skinned tomatoes in a little olive oil, one or two chopped cloves of garlic and a few stoned and chopped black olives. Mix into the pasta, sprinkle over a little chopped basil and serve.

PASTA WITH FENNEL AND PRAWNS

8 oz / 225 g fennel, cut into strips; 4 oz / 120 g shelled prawns; 5 fl oz / 150 ml single cream; clove of garlic, crushed; thinly peeled rind of half a lemon; few fennel leaves.

Simmer the cream and garlic in a small pan very gently for about 12–15 minutes until the cream has thickened slightly and has become perfumed with the garlic. Remove the garlic and set the cream aside. Meanwhile make a *gremolata* by chopping together the lemon rind, a couple of slices of fennel taken from the centre of the bulb and a few fennel leaves. Chop everything as finely as you can and set aside also.

In a large pan of boiling water cook the strips of fennel for 1–2 minutes; they should still be firm and crisp. Remove, drain thoroughly and add to the cream, together with the prawns. Bring the water back to the boil, add olive oil and salt and cook 8 oz / 225 g pasta. Drain and divide between 4 very hot plates. Gently reheat the sauce. Spoon over the pasta, sprinkle with the *gremolata*, and serve immediately with a crisp, dry white wine.

This quantity should serve four as a first course or two as a main course.

PASTA WITH BROAD BEAN PURÉE

Bring a large pan of water to the boil. Add about 12 oz / 340 g fresh broad beans and cook them until they're soft. Remove and blend to a purée with a little of the cooking water, keeping it on the thick side. Enrich with a little butter, season with a scrap of nutmeg and set aside.

Have ready a large carrot cut into *julienne* strips and a similar quantity of celery, also cut into strips. Bring the water back to the boil, add salt and olive oil and cook about 1 lb / 450 g pasta until it is almost cooked. Throw in the carrots and the celery and cook for another 2–3 minutes so that the vegetables are still firm and crisp. (If using fresh pasta, add the vegetables first.) Drain, transfer to a heated serving dish and toss in a tablespoon or so of olive oil. Serve immediately with the broad bean purée spooned over, reheated if necessary.

If it's more convenient, the purée can be made in advance and reheated later. A simple and nutritious dish, particularly nice with wholewheat or semolina pasta.

THUNDER AND LIGHTNING (TUONI E LAMPO)

One can only presume that the rather colourful name of this dish comes from that well-known bean effect. It has always been one of my favourite pasta dishes. Recipes do vary slightly but the basic ingredients are always the same: a roughly equal quantity of cooked chick peas and pasta, mixed together and lubricated with a little olive oil. I use wholewheat pasta and like to flavour the chick peas by frying a savoury mixture of chopped garlic and parsley in the oil and heating the chick peas in this mixture before adding them to the pasta. Sometimes I add a couple of chopped tomatoes as well, or a little *pesto*. One of the best pasta dishes.

PASTA AND CHAKCHOUKA

Chakchouka, a Tunisian dish of stewed peppers and tomatoes with poached eggs, is a natural accompaniment for pasta. The result is a comforting homely sort of dish which makes eating at home the pleasure it is.

approx. 1½ lb / 675 g red or red and green peppers; 1½ lb / 675 g tomatoes; 1 very large sliced onion; 2–3 cloves of garlic, chopped; 2 tablespoons olive oil; dash of basil vinegar (optional); 4 large eggs.

The exact proportions of tomatoes and peppers for this dish can be varied according to taste and supply. I aim for approximately equal quantities of each and, as it reheats and freezes well, it's worth making in quantity. Chop the tomatoes coarsely and cut the peppers into strips, discarding stalks and seeds. In a large, shallow pan soften – don't fry – the onion in the oil until it's no more than lightly coloured. Add the garlic, cook a little longer, then add the tomatoes and peppers. Cook over a moderate heat for 30–40 minutes, or until the stew is thick and well-reduced with no trace of wateriness. Check the seasoning – a dash of basil vinegar perks it up a bit.

Make four hefty depressions in the Chakchouka with the back of a spoon, building up the sides slightly as if you were making a sand castle, and carefully crack an egg into each depression. Cover and cook until the whites have set but the yolks are still runny. Have some wholewheat or semolina pasta ready and waiting. Spoon some of the sauce over each portion of pasta and carefully rest an egg on top. Eat all three, eggs, sauce and pasta together.

Grains   '... it suddenly became clear that all the world's major staple foods ... could comfortably provide all or most of people's daily protein; ... It became clear that instead of growing cereal just to feed cattle and pigs, it would be better simply to eat it.'
COLIN TUDGE, *The Food Connection*, 1985

BULGUR
Bulgur, or cracked wheat as it is sometimes called, is an ancient product eaten extensively in the Middle East, and made by parboiling wholewheat grains in water. These are then spread out to dry in the sun before being cracked into little pieces between stone rollers. Nutritious, with a pleasantly nutty flavour, it requires hardly any cooking, and lends itself to a variety of salads, stuffings and savoury dishes.

BULGUR PILAFF
Bulgur swells up to three times its volume when soaked or cooked, and you should allow for this. Generally speaking, 2–3 oz / 60–90 g per person should be enough. Here the pilaff is intended as the main dish. If you judge you need less, reduce the quantity of bulgur and water but don't worry about the other ingredients – use as little or as much as you like.

12 oz / 340 g bulgur; approx. 24 fl oz / 675 ml water; onion, finely chopped; 1 tablespoon vegetable oil; scant tablespoon soy sauce.

For the savoury mixture: 2 carrots, cut into *julienne* strips; 2–3 tablespoons pine kernels or lightly toasted almond flakes; 2–3 tablespoons raisins; hard-boiled eggs, sliced or quartered; strips of cooked lamb (optional); 1–2 cloves of garlic, cut into thin slivers (optional); little finely chopped parsley; ⅓–½ oz / 10–15 g butter or oil for frying.

In a heavy pan soften the onion until it is well cooked, but not brown, in the oil. Add the wheat, stir it around and cook for a couple of minutes until it begins to smell pleasantly nutty. Add the water and the soy sauce, bring to the boil, cover and cook for a couple of minutes. Remove from the heat and allow the pan to stand for 10 minutes. At the end of this time the wheat will have absorbed all the water and should be soft.

Meanwhile prepare the savoury mixture. The choice of ingredients can be varied, as can the quantity. The idea is to produce a nicely balanced savoury topping which will complement the blandness of the wheat. Begin with the strips of lamb if you're using them, or the carrots if you're not. Melt a knob of butter or a little oil in a pan which will just take all the ingredients and start by frying the meat until it is browned and set aside. Then cook the carrots until they, too, are nicely browned. Add the raisins and pine kernels (the almonds are kept separate and sprinkled over last), followed by the garlic. Stir everything frequently so that nothing burns. The whole operation shouldn't take more than 5–10 minutes. Fluff the wheat lightly with a fork and cover the top with the savoury mixture. Decorate with hard-boiled eggs, sprinkle with a little parsley if you have it, and serve immediately with vegetables or salad and a bowl of plain yoghurt.

For a slighter drier dish, reduce the quantity of water, using one and a half times the amount of water to dried weight of bulgur. This is the proportion I prefer.

CARROT AND BULGUR QUICKIE

Pour boiling water over as much cracked wheat as you want and let it stand for 5 minutes to swell and soften. Cook an equal volume of 'strawed' carrots as on p. 66. Drain the soaked wheat, pressing out the excess moisture, add to the carrots, stir, cook another couple of minutes to heat through, and serve. You can add a hard-boiled egg and some fresh herbs, though I must confess I find it most acceptable on its own.

MEYDIHA'S KISIR
A Wheat Dish from Turkey

A recipe from *The Anthropologist's Cookbook*, edited by Jessica Kuper for the Royal Anthropological Society. The recipe was given to Marianne and Jerry Leach by Meydiha, one of the villagers who lived outside the city of Medana.

8 oz / 225 g bulgur; 6 spring onions, including tops, finely chopped; 1 clove of garlic, finely chopped, 2 tablespoons mild olive oil; 20 fl oz / 600 ml boiling water; 1 teaspoon tomato purée or 1 tablespoon fresh tomato sauce; 2–4 oz / 60–120 g finely chopped parsley, preferably the flat type; juice of 1–2 lemons; salt, pepper, cayenne (in Turkey, chilli pepper pulp would be used), to taste. Romaine or cos lettuce leaves and quarters of lemon for serving.

Gently sweat the onions and garlic in the oil until soft. Add the cracked wheat and stir until well mixed. Add the tomato purée or sauce and boiling water, cover and cook gently until all the water has been absorbed. This should take no more than 4–5 minutes. The wheat expands and becomes soft and fluffy. Stir in the parsley, lemon juice and seasonings to taste. Allow the dish to stand covered for a further 5–10 minutes to let the flavours mingle and be absorbed.

The authors recommend serving the *kisir* on a large platter in the centre of the table. Place two or three bowls of chilled lemon quarters around the table, together with small bowls of lettuce for each person. 'People should spoon the wheat from the platter with the lettuce, adding a dash of lemon juice before eating.' Leftovers can be successfully reheated adding a little extra water.

BULGUR AND POMEGRANATE JUICE

In Southern Turkey sour pomegranate juice, rather than lemon juice, is used in *tabbouleh*, a salad made by soaking bulgur in water, squeezing it dry and, lastly, adding lemon juice, oil, spring onions and a lot of parsley to colour it green. I have found this excellent. As pomegranates here tend to be sweet, sharpen with lemon juice. Use the juice of 2 or 3 pomegranates with lemon juice to taste and fork in some pomegranate seeds. They add colour and provide a contrast to the softness of the wheat. A lovely dish which tastes as good as it looks.

Try pomegranates in *Meydiha's kisir* also.

SAVOURY MILLET

It's a pity that millet is known principally as bird food, for it has an agreeable sweetish flavour which blends well with vegetables and makes a more than acceptable change from bulgur.

12 oz / 340 g millet; approx. 24 fl oz / 675 ml water; 1 tablespoon soy sauce; medium onion, finely chopped; 2–3 large sticks of celery, diced; 1 fresh chilli, seeds removed and chopped; 4 oz / 120 g frozen peas; 1 tablespoon vegetable oil.

Gently sweat the onion, celery and chilli in a heavy pan until soft. Stir in the millet, cook for a minute until the grains smell pleasantly nutty. Add the soy sauce, peas and water, bring to the boil, cover, and cook over a very gentle heat until all the water has been absorbed, 15 minutes or so. Turn off the heat and leave for another 10 minutes. The millet will continue to cook in its own steam and absorb the flavour of the vegetables. It's ready when the grains are beginning to burst and are soft but still a little crunchy. Fluff up and serve with other vegetables and salads rather than meat. If you like your peas bright green, cook them separately and add them at the end.

BUCKWHEAT PANCAKES

Easy, and less trouble than *blinis*.

For 8 small pancakes: 4 oz / 120 g ricotta or cottage cheese; 2 oz / 60 g buckwheat flour; 1 beaten egg; 1 egg white, stiffly beaten.
To finish (see method): sour cream/ordinary cream/*quark*/thick yoghurt; tomato sauce or chopped fresh tomatoes; strips of smoked salmon or other smoked fish; fresh chopped herbs – dill, chives, chervil, sorrel; cooked beetroot.

Simply beat the first three ingredients to a stiff dropping consistency and then fold in the well beaten egg white. The mixture should be fairly stiff, thicker than an ordinary pancake but lighter in texture. Heat a lightly greased heavy pan over a low heat, and when it's hot, place a heaped tablespoon of the mixture in the centre. It will spread just a little. Cook until bubbles appear on the surface, keeping the heat very low. This should only take 2 or 3 minutes. Flick the pancake over and cook the other side briefly. Keep warm while you make the other pancakes in the same way. Use a largish pan or two together and cook two or more pancakes at a time. Re-greasing the pan should not be necessary.

The pancakes can be served in any number of ways: begin by

spreading each with a little sour cream/ordinary cream/thick yoghurt or *quark* let down with a little milk. Add a spoonful of tomato sauce or fresh tomatoes chopped to a pulp and finish with herbs; or add strips of smoked fish and decorate with the appropriate herb; or some finely chopped cooked beetroot seasoned, perhaps, with a pinch of caraway seeds set on a blob of sour cream; or simply cover with chopped chives and dill. These are savoury little mouthfuls and a splendid first course.

Pulses   *Beans and cereals keep Africans, Chinese, Indians and Mexicans alive. Not just alive; they also keep them in good health . . . Britain needs more beans.*
CAROLINE WALKER and GEOFFREY CANNON
The Food Scandal, 1984

CASSOULET
A glorious dish. It requires a stout appetite, a cold day and not much on the agenda afterwards. The sort of dish worth walking 10 miles for.

12–16 oz / 340–450 g haricot beans; approx. 1¼ lb / 570 g each of lean shoulder of lamb and pork; 4–6 oz / 120–170 g green bacon bought in a piece and cut into tiny rectangular dice; large onion stuck with 2 cloves; 2 fat cloves of garlic, crushed and chopped; 2 tomatoes, quartered; 2 sprigs parsley; fine, dry breadcrumbs, white or brown.

Soak the beans in the usual way, either overnight or by boiling them for 5 minutes and then leaving them to soak for a couple of hours. Drain and rinse in fresh water. Put them in a pan with the onion, cover with fresh water and gently cook on the top of the stove for 40 minutes.

Remove the rind from the pork and cut both the pork and the lamb into sizeable chunks. Put them to roast in a hot oven until the outside surfaces are brown. Do this while the beans are cooking.

Choose a large, deep casserole dish and put in a layer of beans with some of the onion and one of the tomatoes. Next add the partly roasted meat, and over that scatter the garlic and diced bacon. Finish with the rest of the beans, onion and tomato. Pour in the juices from the roasting tin, adding enough of the cooking water from the beans barely to cover. Place the pork rind on top and bury the parsley. Bring to the boil, cover loosely and transfer to the lowest oven possible to cook very gently for anything up to 4 hours. It's the long, slow cooking that makes this dish, so check from time to time that everything is as it should be. Remove from the oven when the meat is very tender and the beans are soft as butter. Remove the pork rind and soak up all the fat which will be swimming on top with kitchen paper. Leave the cassoulet overnight.

Next day, check the level of the liquid. If it seems too copious, remove some. Otherwise cover the top with a thick layer of breadcrumbs and cook, uncovered this time, in a moderately hot oven for about another hour until the surface is nicely crisped and browned. Serve with a light red wine and bread to mop up the juices. Something like a fresh pineapple to follow and nothing more adventurous than a green salad beforehand. [Serves 4–6.]

MRS BEETON'S POTTED BEANS
A very different recipe from the previous one. I found it in Mrs Beeton's *Shilling Cookery*, published in 1904. The ingredients as Mrs Beeton gave them:

½ pint (8 oz) haricot beans; 2 oz grated breadcrumbs; 2 oz strong cheese, grated; 2 oz butter; cayenne, pepper, salt and nutmeg to taste.

Soak and cook the beans in the usual way and drain off the cooking liquid. Mrs Beeton then set to and pounded the beans by hand, gradually incorporating the rest of the ingredients. These days everything can be done in seconds in a blender or food processor. The mixture should be smooth and stiffish. Add seasoning to taste and pot into individual ramekin dishes. This quantity will fill about eight, so you may want to try half quantities first. The result is something between a pâté and a spread. In 1904 it cost 5d to make. Serve as a first course with salad and brown bread and eat within two or three days of making.

Don't be afraid to adapt the recipe. My preference is for blue cheese and less butter, and I find that using half her quantity of breadcrumbs makes for a creamier texture.

SPICED LENTILS
A rich, warm-flavoured dish which goes admirably well with pheasant or smoked pork, or on its own with hard-boiled eggs and vegetables such as spinach. It reheats successfully and can be puréed if preferred.

8 oz / 225 g whole brown lentils, picked over; 1 onion, chopped; big sprig of thyme; slice of unsmoked bacon; 1 inch / 2.5 cm stick of cinnamon; 2–3 cloves; piece of dried orange rind; 1 pint / 600 ml game stock; pinch of grated nutmeg; butter for frying.

Melt a knob of butter in a pan, add the bacon and onion and gently cook for about 5 minutes, stirring occasionally. Add the rest of the ingredients, cover and continue cooking over a low heat until the lentils are tender and creamy, adding a little more stock or water as necessary. Fish out the bacon, thyme stalks and orange rind and, if you wish, the whole spices and serve. [Serves 4 as a side dish.]

LENTILS AND WINE
Sweat a finely chopped onion in a knob of butter, add 8 oz / 225 g lentils – brown or the lovely slate-green Puy lentils are best for this dish – a bouquet garni and enough water to cover. Cook until the lentils are tender, adding more water as necessary. Remove the bouquet garni and, just before serving, stir in up to a glass of medium sweet white wine, enough to taste without the flavour dominating. A lump of butter can also be added.

The wine has a cheering effect on the lentils and a warming effect on the stomach. Another good dish for game, especially the strong flavoured sort. [Serves 4 as a side dish.]

FAGIOLI CON TONNO
One of the very best store-cupboard salads.

8 oz / 225 g cooked Italian pinto beans (allow 4 oz / 120 g uncooked weight); 8 oz / 225 g can of tuna fish; few paper-thin slivers of onion; 1–2 tablespoons olive oil; 2 stoned, halved and finely sliced black olives (optional); little finely chopped parsley (optional).

Soak and cook the beans in the usual way – they take about an hour. Drain, rinse in clean water, and toss in olive oil while still warm. Drain the oil from the tuna and gently mix with the beans, being careful not to break it up too much nor to mix too thoroughly. The tuna should remain in discernible lumps. Transfer to a serving bowl and decorate with slivers of onion. Neither the olives nor the parsley is authentic but they both look and taste well with the salad. Salt shouldn't be necessary as the canned tuna will provide plenty but check the taste to see. Serve as a first course with pitta bread or as part of a mixed hors d'oeuvres.

TWO-BEAN SALAD
An Armenian salad I have grown fond of in the last couple of years. The two beans are runner beans and kidney beans, although it can be made equally successfully with french beans and kidney beans. It makes a

most marvellous splash of colour and is one of those salads which is almost a meal in itself.

8 oz / 225 g cooked kidney beans (allow 4 oz / 120 g uncooked weight); 8 oz / 225 g sliced runner or french beans; 2 tablespoons chopped spring onion; quartered hard-boiled eggs.

For the dressing: 1 oz / 30 g walnuts; 1 tablespoon wine vinegar; 3–4 tablespoons water; 1 tablespoon each of finely chopped parsley and coriander; clove of garlic, crushed and chopped; pinch of salt.

Cook the kidney beans in the usual way, drain and rinse in fresh water to remove any muddiness. Blanch the green beans in a large pan of boiling water for 1–2 minutes depending on how thickly you have sliced them. They should be just cooked and very crunchy. Drain and set aside. Blend the walnuts, wine vinegar, garlic and water in a blender or a food processor to a smooth cream and add salt to taste. Set aside a few of each of the beans and the hard-boiled eggs as garnish. Combine all the ingredients in a large bowl, mixing thoroughly. Transfer to a serving dish, decorate with the reserved beans and hard-boiled eggs and keep in a cool place until required.

Sweet and Simple

True gourmets always have finished their meal before the sweet. All that they eat later is by politeness, but gourmets are usually very polite.

GRIMOD DE LA REYNIÈRE in *Gambols in Gastronomy* by William Wallace Irwin, 1960

Sweet things are a problem, the stickiest dilemma of all. Cookery books are of little help. They invite us to indulge in orgies of cream and sugar, offer no tempting alternatives, no word of caution.

This need not be so. It is possible to satisfy the need for sweetness, but in a more responsible way. Fresh fruit makes marvellous desserts as well as providing a bonus of vitamins, minerals and fibre. And it offers so much choice: a fresh fruit salad, arranged attractively on a plate with a swirl of contrasting purée, a frothy fruit *sabayon*, blackcurrant flummery or gooseberry tansy, soufflés, sorbets, whips and jellies, exotically perfumed dried fruit salads, a bowl of summer fruits, warm and fragrant. What could be nicer than a ripe, juicy pear, a crisp English Cox's apple, a bunch of cherries, or a plump dessert gooseberry, heavy with scent and pregnant with sweetness? Nor need our traditional puddings be cast aside. With a little imagination and judicious substitution – lighter sponges, yoghurt-based fools and ice creams, foamy egg sauces – many possibilities soon become apparent.

In the recipes that follow sugar and cream have been kept to a minimum with just enough to supplement the natural sweetness of fruits, or to give a dessert the desired creamy feel. At all times this should be your aim, but be prepared to adjust slightly up or down as seems appropriate. In an ideal world we would, I'm sure, do away with puddings and desserts. Nutritionally, it makes sense. At least let us try to lay down sounder foundations for a healthier, less sugary future.

ALMOND TARTLETS

This recipe is one of Mrs Myrtle Allen's who runs one restaurant at Ballymaloe, near Cork and another in Paris. They are delightfully dainty cases for fresh fruit. This quantity makes about a dozen. Allow two per person.

Cream together 2 oz / 60 g each of softened butter, ground almonds and caster sugar. Drop teaspoons of the mixture into ungreased, individual tartlet tins or those baking tins used for small cakes. Pat them lightly with the fingers to make them smooth and even. Bake in a moderate oven, 180°C / 350°F / gas mark 4, for about 10 minutes until golden brown. (Until you've made a few timing can be tricky, so it's wise to cook a trial batch first.) Let them settle and cool a little to firm up, then remove with a palette knife to finish cooling on a rack. On no account let them cool in their tins as they become brittle and are likely to break.

Choose fruit such as fresh strawberries, cherries or peaches, and arrange neatly in the tartlets. Spoon over a little appropriate glaze or a tiny blob of whipped cream, and serve immediately before the fruit has time to soften the crisp case. Store any remaining in a covered box in the refrigerator.

ANDALUSIAN WHIM-WHAM

I first made this during a brief visit to Spain, using local Malaga wine and raisins and beautifully sweet and juicy oranges. It was delicious. At home you will need to use the ingredients to hand, so adapt and improvise as you see fit. The charm of the dish lies in the combination of three different tastes and textures – a hot orange custard, a smooth, wine-soaked sponge and crunchy, sweet raisins.

Per person: 1 dessertspoon large muscatel raisins; small slice of plain Madeira or similar cake; 2–3 tablespoons marsala or sweet sherry.

For the custard (enough for 4): 3 medium egg yolks; 10 fl oz / 300 ml freshly squeezed and strained orange juice (approx. 4 large, juicy oranges); a little soft brown sugar if necessary.

Choose 4 fairly tall, robust glasses. Soak the raisins in boiling water for a few minutes to soften, drain, and put a few in the bottom of each glass. Moisten with a little of the fortified wine. Cut the cake so it will just fit the shape of the glasses snugly and push into place on top of the raisins.

Pour over the rest of the marsala or sherry, cover with cling film and put in the oven to heat through. You want them nice and hot. Beat the orange juice and egg yolks together in a basin over a pan of gently simmering water until the custard is hot and creamy, 7–10 minutes. Sweeten if necessary, but keep it on the sharp side bearing in mind the sweetness of the other elements. Fill the glasses with custard and serve immediately.

APPLE OR PEAR PUDDING

A favourite of mine – as comforting as a cake but light as a soufflé.

2 large eggs, separated; rind and juice of 1 large lemon; 1 oz / 30 g soft brown sugar; 1 dessertspoon caster sugar; 1 oz / 30 g melted and cooled butter; 1½ oz / 45 g sifted flour; 2 ripe eating pears or 2 medium eating apples.

Using a pastry brush and a little of the melted butter, coat the bottom and sides of an 1½ pint / 850 ml soufflé dish and set aside. Peel, core, and quarter the fruit, and slice each quarter into very thin slices. Whisk together the egg yolks, brown sugar and lemon juice until thick and light. Add the sifted flour, whisk again to incorporate thoroughly. Finally stir in the melted butter, finely grated rind and fruit. In a separate bowl, whisk the egg whites to the soft peak stage. Add the caster sugar and continue whisking until stiff and shiny. Gently but thoroughly fold the two mixtures together and transfer to the prepared dish. Stand the dish in a tray containing water and bake in a moderately hot oven 180–190°C / 350–375°F / gas mark 4–5, for about 50–60 minutes, protecting the top with greaseproof paper when sufficiently browned.

Timing can be a bit tricky. Test after 50 minutes with a skewer. If the cake is still very moist, give it another 5–10 minutes until the centre is just cooked. Allow to cool slightly and serve from the same dish. Sufficient for four small servings.

APPLE MERINGUE

1½ lb / 675 g dessert or sweetish cooking apple such as Lord Derby; 1–2 oz / 30–60 g soft brown sugar; rind of 1 lemon, finely grated; 2 egg yolks.

For the meringue: 2 egg whites; 2 oz / 60 g caster sugar; 1–2 oz / 30–60 g flaked or ground almonds.

Peel, core, and slice the apples and cook in a little water with the lemon rind until soft and pulpy. Cool slightly, beat to a purée, sweeten to taste and mix in the egg yolks. Transfer to a shallow pudding dish making sure there's ample room left for the meringue topping. The apple mixture can be left at this stage until later.

Whisk the egg whites until just stiff, add half the sugar and whisk again until the mixture is very thick and shiny. Fold in the rest of the sugar, keeping back a teaspoon or so. Carefully spoon the meringue over the apple mixture in uneven blobs, sprinkle with the reserved sugar and scatter almonds over the surface.

Cook briefly in a moderate hot oven until the top is golden brown, then turn the oven down to very low and continue cooking for another 45 minutes or so, protecting the top with greaseproof paper. You should end up with a nicely crisped, moist and well puffed meringue which doesn't run or collapse. Serve warm or cold.

LA TARTE DES DEMOISELLES TATIN

An excellent variation – instead of the usual shortcrust base, the caramelised apples sit on a light, fatless sponge.

For a 7 in / 18 cm base: 1 lb / 450 g eating apples, e.g. Cox; rind of 1 lemon, finely grated; 1 oz / 30 g unsalted butter; 1½–2 oz / 45–60 g caster sugar; Calvados or brandy.

For the sponge: 2 eggs, weighed (approx. 5 oz / 150 g); 2½ oz / 75 g each of caster sugar and sifted plain flour, or half wheatmeal and half plain flour sifted together; few drops of vanilla essence.

Choose a heavy-based pan or dish which can be used on top of the stove and in the oven with sides a good 1 in / 2.5 cm deep. A le Creuset gratin dish is ideal. Spread half the butter over the base and cover thickly with sugar. Peel, core, and quarter the apples, and slice each quarter into thickish slices. Arrange these in concentric circles over the base, overlapping slightly. Dredge with the remaining sugar, sprinkle over the lemon rind and dot the remaining butter, cut into tiny pieces, over the whole. Set over a high heat and cook, undisturbed, until the butter and sugar have formed a rich brown caramel and the apples are tender but not collapsed. This will take 10–15 minutes. Leave to cool.

Next make the sponge. Weigh the eggs, then weigh out half their weight in sugar and flour. Place the eggs, sugar and vanilla essence in a large bowl over a pan of hot water and whisk with an electric whisk until very thick and foamy and the beater leaves a firm trail in the pale yellow foam. Remove the pan from the heat and continue whisking for a little while longer, to incorporate as much air as possible. Lightly but thoroughly fold in the sifted flour and spread the mixture over the cooled apples. Cook on a baking sheet in a preheated oven at 190°C / 375°F / gas mark 5 for 25–30 minutes until the sponge is golden brown and firm to the touch. The *tatin* needs to be turned out straightaway. Slip a palette knife around the edges to loosen, invert a round serving plate on top and, using oven gloves to protect your hands, quickly turn the two upside down. The cake should come away cleanly but you may need to replace any stubborn pieces of apple. Swill the pan out with a lavish measure of Calvados or brandy scraping up all the caramelly bits, pour over the top of the cake and serve warm or cold but not chilled. If you want a larger cake, say a 9 in / 23 cm base, use a three-egg sponge and up to double the quantities of apple etc.

APRICOT AND ALMOND TATIN
A variation of the above, and very good. Substitute for the apples enough soaked and strained Hunza apricots (the wild apricots from Afghanistan, available from health food stores) to cover the base. Instead of lemon rind, crack the stones to get at the kernels and scatter these over the apricots. Use a little almond essence instead of vanilla for the sponge. Deglaze the pan after cooking with Grand Marnier or Amaretto liqueur.

GRILLED BANANAS
A messy dish with an incomparable flavour. Well spotted, ripe bananas are essential, so choose with care. Place your banana, unpeeled, on a tin or in a fire-proof dish and grill under a hot grill for about 7–10 minutes, during which the skin will blacken and the juice ooze out to form its own delicious sauce. Tear off a strip of skin and eat with a spoon, not forgetting to scrape up all the sauce. The dish can be made more presentable by serving it on a warmed plate and glazing it with a little apricot or strawberry jam – the kind of refinement I suspect we bother with for other people but rarely for ourselves.

BANANAS POACHED IN ORANGE AND CARDAMOM SAUCE
Josceline Dimbleby first introduced this exquisitely fragrant sauce for bananas. Mine is merely a simpler variation.

Allow half a large ripe banana per person. Peel, slice down the middle and cut each half into two. Extract the seeds from 4 or more cardamom pods and crush in a mortar and pestle. Put the bananas and cardamom seeds in a small pan and barely cover with a mixture of concentrated orange juice, diluted with 2–3 tablespoons of water. Poach very gently for about 5 minutes until the bananas are soft. They take on a brilliant marigold orange-yellow. Serve immediately with a little of the sauce spooned over. No sugar is required, the concentrated orange juice has more than enough.

BANANA IN YOGHURT CUSTARD
Make a yoghurt custard according to the directions on p. 169. When it's almost ready add about half a large ripe banana per person, peeled and sliced into thick chunks. Let the bananas get hot and soften slightly and serve immediately. Delicious.

BANANA SNOWBALL
A first class idea which came originally from a slimming magazine. It's a sort of ice cold instant whip but far superior to the packet kind and ideal for children. It contains no sugar and takes two minutes to make.

2 peaches; 1 large ripe banana; approx. 4 tablespoons orange juice or other fruit juice.

Dice the fruit into 1 in / 2.5 cm chunks and freeze in a container until solid, about two hours. Transfer to a food processor, add the fruit juice and process until smooth. At first it makes an alarming noise but soon the mixture transforms into a creamy, peach-coloured, foamy mass. Spoon into glasses and serve immediately. Almost any fruit combination you can think of works with this recipe. Choose fruit with bulk such as pineapple or banana and combine with others of your choice.

FRUITS-IN-BATTER PUDDING
Whatever happened to our batter puddings which abound in old cook books? This one is French. They have the sense to hang on to the best of their simple things. It's a dried fruit version of its more famous sister *clafoutis*, and comes from the Times-Life *Good Cook* series, edited by Richard Olney, author also of this recipe. Easy and adaptable, it works well with both fresh and dried fruit, my particular favourite being a mixture of dried figs and fresh cherries. I have reduced the quantities slightly and made minor changes.

1½ oz / 45 g sultanas or raisins; 6 oz / 170 g prunes (or dried figs or apricots) or 6 oz / 170 g fresh fruit such as cherries, pears or peaches; 3 fl oz / 90 ml brandy or other appropriate spirit; 2 oz / 60 g soft brown sugar; 1½ oz / 45 g sifted flour, brown or white; 3 eggs; approx. 6 fl oz / 180 ml milk; ½ teaspoon vanilla essence; butter for greasing.

Wash fresh fruit and pour boiling water over the dried and leave for 10 minutes to soften. Halve the prunes and stone. Slice, chop and stone other fruit as appropriate and leave to macerate in the alcohol for at least 4 hours (longer if possible for dried fruit), turning often.

Beat the eggs and sugar with a balloon whisk and add the sifted flour, a little at a time, whisking well after each addition. Add the fruit and its juice, the vanilla essence and enough milk to make a thin batter. (Dried fruit will soak up more of the alcohol, fresh fruit less.) Spoon into a lightly buttered, shallow earthenware or porcelain dish and bake in a fairly hot oven, 200°C / 400°F / gas mark 6, for 20–25 minutes until nicely brown and puffed up. The centre should be just set. Serve, lukewarm, from the same dish.

BLACKCURRANT FLUMMERY

Flummery is a lovely name for a dessert and better, it has to be said, than the dish itself which was traditionally a cream-like sweet, thickened with the liquid from soaked oatmeal and sweetened with honey. This is a modern variation taken, with minor changes, from Margaret Costa's *Four Seasons' Cookery Book*. Try and use *crème de cassis* if you can. With all these fruit-based desserts, a little of the appropriate spirit or liqueur lifts them a little. A simple but elegant and richly-flavoured dessert.

1 lb / 450 g blackcurrants (frozen are fine); 1 tablespoon cornflour; 5 fl oz / 150 ml water; 2–3 oz / 60–90 g sugar; 1–2 teaspoons lemon juice; 2 tablespoons *crème de cassis* (optional).

To finish: pearly currants (p. 161); *crème de cassis* or single cream.

Soften the blackcurrants in the water over a low heat. Sieve to extract all the purée and return to the pan. Sweeten to taste, keeping on the sharp side. Mix the cornflour with a little water, add to the rest of the mixture and boil gently for two minutes, stirring constantly. Add lemon juice to taste followed by the *crème de cassis*. Spoon into small individual glasses, dust with caster sugar to prevent a skin from forming and chill until required. Just before serving – and not before, otherwise the cream will curdle and the *cassis* sink to the bottom – decorate with a sprig of pearly currants and spoon a thin film of *crème de cassis* or single cream over the surface.

Blackcurrants vary in juiciness. Should the sieved purée be exceedingly thick, dilute with a little extra water.

CHESTNUT MOUSSE

In her *Gentle Art of Cookery* first published in 1925, Mrs Leyel devotes a whole chapter to chestnuts. These days we are lucky to find any. It's a sign, I think, not so much of changing tastes but more of changes of another kind. We are busier now, time is at a premium, and kitchen help has long gone. It's our loss. Chestnuts are blessed with a natural sweetness and creamy, mellow richness. They make excellent desserts.

1 lb / 450 g chestnuts; 2 tablespoons caster sugar; 2 tablespoons brandy; 1 teaspoon vanilla sugar; 2 egg whites; 2–4 fl oz / 60–120 ml whipping cream; milk to cover.

To finish: tiny, fresh or sugared mint leaves or chocolate curls.

Boil the chestnuts in water for 15 minutes. Drain and, when they are cool enough to handle, slice in half and scoop out the flesh, transferring it to a small pan. You should get at least 8 oz / 225 g in weight. Add the vanilla sugar and enough milk to cover and simmer gently until the chestnuts are very soft. Blend in a blender or food processor until smooth as velvet. If the purée seems at all loose, return to the pan and continue cooking until it is good and thick. Set aside until cold.

Whip the egg whites until frothy, add the sugar gradually and continue whisking until the mixture is stiff and shiny. Stir the brandy into the purée and carefully incorporate the egg whites. Chill until required. Just before serving, whip the cream and fold lightly into the mousse-like mixture. How much cream depends on how much mixture the chestnuts made and on individual taste. Spoon into champagne or other pretty glasses, decorate and serve immediately.

CHERRY SABAYON

8–10 oz / 225–280 g fresh cherries, washed, stoned and halved; 2 egg yolks; scant 2 oz / 50 g caster sugar; 3–4 fl oz / 90–120 ml medium sweet white wine, German or Italian preferably; Kirsch.

Fill 4 tall, fluted glasses half full of cherries and sprinkle over a little Kirsch. Cover with cling film and put in a low oven to heat through. While they're heating make the *sabayon*. Whisk the egg yolks, sugar and wine until thick and foamy over a pan of hot water, using an electric whisk. Keep whisking until the *sabayon* is hot and mousse-like. Add a little extra Kirsch, divide between the 4 glasses and serve immediately whilst everything is nice and hot.

PEARLY CURRANTS

A lovely decorative idea, simplicity itself, which I found in *Good French Cooking* by Mapie, alias la Comtesse Guy de Toulouse-Lautrec.

In a small pan make a syrup of 1 oz / 30 g sugar and 2 tablespoons of water and boil gently until it begins to thicken. Allow to cool slightly and then take small bunches of ripe black, red or white currants and dip them, one at a time, into the syrup. Shake off all the excess and lightly roll each bunch in caster sugar and lay on a rack to dry. This quantity of syrup, though small, should be enough for about 8 bunches of fruit, but it's a simple matter to increase the quantity according to your needs. Should the syrup thicken too much as it gets progressively cooler, dilute with a teaspoon of water and reheat gently.

The sugar dries to a crisp, frosted coating. Enjoy the berries as they are or use them as decoration, draped over glasses or arranged on a plate to garnish fresh fruits and sorbets.

DRIED FIGS IN WINE

A favourite store cupboard recipe. For best results, make at least one day before you need it.

Allow three large or four small figs per person. Pour boiling water over them and allow to stand for 5 minutes to soften a little. Drain and arrange in a pan, preferably one in which you can fit them all in a single layer. Pour in enough red wine – or two thirds wine and one third water – to submerge them completely, and poach gently with the lid slightly ajar for about 30 minutes or until the figs are very soft. Leave to stand overnight or longer if you can.

To serve, pinch each fig with your fingers to restore their original shape. Bring them gently back to the boil, transfer to warmed shallow serving dishes and keep warm. Now taste and consider the sauce. It should be sweet and rich but will vary slightly in consistency depending on how generous a measure of wine you used, and how long the figs were left to stand. If you feel it is right, spoon around the figs and serve. Alternatively, reduce further or thicken with a little arrowroot slaked in water and cooked for 2–3 minutes to clear. Food for the gods, which happens to be good for you as well. Equally delicious hot or cold.

PRUNE WHIP

Cook 8 oz / 225 g of prunes as directed on p. 159, keeping the purée very thick. Add about two thirds its volume of either *quark* or very thick yoghurt and taste to see if it requires any sugar. It should be an agreeable chocolate colour, mottled rather than even. Spoon into individual glasses and chill until required. Just before serving, dust with a little brown cinnamon sugar, made by mixing a dessertspoon of sugar with a teaspoon of powdered cinnamon. A delicious sweet but rich. Serve in small portions in pretty glasses.

GOOSEBERRY FOOL

I would rather have a ripe and fragrant dessert gooseberry – a Whitesmith or a Leveller – than almost any other fruit. Such luxuries are hard to come by unless you grow your own so we must settle instead for the next best thing, gooseberry fool. Quintessentially English, there is no definitive recipe, only individual preferences. Mine is for gooseberries, cream and sugar. Traditional recipes call for hard, green gooseberries. Should there be a choice, go for ripe gooseberries which need less cooking and less sugar.

1 lb / 450 g green or sweet dessert gooseberries; 2–3 oz / 60–90 g sugar; approx. 5 fl oz / 150 ml whipping cream; 1–2 drops of green food colouring (optional).

Cook the gooseberries very gently with a tablespoon of water in a covered pan until they soften. Ripe gooseberries will hardly need any cooking, unripe gooseberries about 5–7 minutes. Drain off any excess juice. Either crush the gooseberries with a fork, or pass through the coarse mill of a *mouli*. This removes the worst of the pips. Sweeten to taste, but keep on the sharp side. Now, measure the pulp. There should be about ½ pint / 300 ml. Set aside to cool.

At this point, I add a single drop or, at the most, two drops of food colouring. With red gooseberries such as London Pride, such unnatural practices are uncalled for, the cooked gooseberries are a beautiful dark-pink but others turn a yellow-grey and a drop of colouring helps.

Ripe gooseberries tend to produce less pulp so add a few extra fresh ones, chopped into small pieces to bring up to the required volume. Measure out half the quantity of cream to fruit and whip until it will just hold its shape. Very lightly – barely at all – fold the two mixtures together, leaving the fool mottled rather than even in colour. Spoon into small stemmed glasses and chill until required.

GOOSEBERRY TANSY

Tansy is a sort of egg custard or sweetened flat omelette, depending on how it's made. It is an ancient dish, dating right back to the Middle Ages, and named after the pungent herb used to colour it green. This was dropped as a flavouring early in the eighteenth century but the dish has retained its name. It's a simple, homely dish, easily made and popular with children. Mine is an adaptation, but in the eighteenth-century style.

1 lb / 450 g gooseberries; 2 oz / 60 g soft brown sugar; 1–2 teaspoons rose or orange flower water; 1 tablespoon sherry; 2 whole eggs plus 2 egg yolks; 1–2 oz / 30–60 g soft white or brown breadcrumbs; ¼ oz / 7–8 g butter.

Cook the gooseberries in the butter over a gentle heat until soft and collapsed. Cool slightly, sweeten to taste, keeping the flavour on the sharp side, and beat in the eggs. Add other seasonings to taste and enough breadcrumbs to bind the mixture together lightly. Cook very gently over a low heat until thick and creamy, adding a few extra breadcrumbs if it seems too wet. As with any egg mixture, don't let it boil. You will get no thanks for scrambled tansy. Spoon into warm glasses and serve immediately.

Alternatively cook the mixture as you would a flat omelette. Stiffen with extra breadcrumbs and cook in the usual way, finishing it off under the grill. This is more orthodox, though I cannot say I have had much success with it myself, and prefer the creaminess of the first version.

HEISS HIMBEER

Why have we no recipes for hot raspberries? In Germany, *Heiss Himbeer* can be found on the menu of most small-town Gasthofs. It makes one of the best winter desserts I know, ideal for those supplies of frozen raspberries horded away during summer.

Thaw out a generous helping of raspberries per person. Tip into a pan, sweeten to taste – about a dessertspoon of sugar per person should be about right – and cook very gently for 3–4 minutes until the fruit is very hot, the juices have begun to run and some of the raspberries have disintegrated to form a sauce. Serve immediately in hot fruit bowls.

KHOSAF

Khosaf, the Middle-Eastern salad of dried fruit perfumed with flower water, has to be one of the most delicious ways of eating fibre possible. I often wonder why traditional recipes all contain so much sugar for dried fruit is packed full of it. This version does not.

8 large prunes; generous 4 oz / 120 g Hunza apricots, or a mixture of dried apricots and small dried figs; 1 tablespoon raisins; 1 tablespoon each of pine kernels and blanched, halved almonds; 1 tablespoon rose water; 1 tablespoon orange flower water; 1 dessertspoon soft brown sugar.

To finish: 1 fresh orange, cut into segments, pith and skin removed, or a few pomegranate seeds.

Start by pouring boiling water over the fruit to clean it and to help remove any mineral oil and preservatives. Drain and put into a deep bowl with all the other ingredients. Add enough water to cover the fruit, cover and leave in a cool place for at least 48 hours. As the fruit macerates in the liquid it transforms it to a sweet and fragrant sauce. To serve, distribute the fruit between four dishes and add either the pomegranate seeds or a few slices of fresh orange to each dish, saving any juice to add to the sauce. Spoon the sauce around the fruit and serve.

Khosaf is worth making in large quantities and keeps easily for a week or more. A fine winter dessert.

STUFFED HOT NECTARINES OR PEACHES

Wash the fruit if necessary, halve, stone and lay side by side in a shallow ovenproof dish. Mix together a savoury mixture of ricotta or other soft cheese, with a little chopped citrus peel, a few finely chopped, unblanched almonds or hazel nuts or, if these are not available, a crumbled macaroon biscuit, an optional pinch of cinnamon or ground allspice, and flavour with a dash of Amaretto, Grand Marnier or brandy. Fill the cavities with the mixture, smoothing it out to form a neat dome shape, and grill under a moderately hot grill until hot and the surface has lightly browned. Serve immediately.

CARAMELLED ORANGES
A simple, fresh version. One of the best sweets after a heavy meal.

4 large juicy oranges; 2 scant tablespoons sugar; 2 tablespoons water; 2 tablespoons Grand Marnier.

Scrub the oranges in hot water. Remove the peel with a lemon zester in hair-like strands and poach these in water for about 15 minutes to soften. Drain and set aside. Meanwhile prepare the oranges. Using a sharp, serrated knife cut away all the pith and cut the segments away from their membrane. Take out any pips and set aside. Squeeze all the juice from the debris and set aside also. To make the caramel, put the sugar and water into a small pan, stir to dissolve the sugar and cook over a moderate heat until it begins to brown and to smell like caramel. Up to this point it needs little attention. Now watch it like a hawk – as soon as it has developed a good colour take it off the heat immediately. Add the rind – it will sizzle furiously, and become a translucent, golden brown. Let it cool for 5 minutes or so, stir in the orange juice and leave the caramel to dissolve in the juice, about 2–3 hours.

Choose shallow fruit dishes and arrange the orange slices in a star-shaped pattern. Place a little heap of rind in the centre, add the Grand Marnier to the juice and spoon over the oranges. Chill, protected with cling film until required.

PEAR, PERSIMMON AND LYCHEE SALAD
Fruit salads are no longer chopped up, drowned in syrup and confined to a bowl. Now we try to show off each slice of fruit, emphasise the natural curves and colours, and keep embellishments to a minimum.

There are no recipes, no do's and don'ts. All you need is some fresh fruit and a little imagination.

Purée one large or two smaller persimmons in a blender, sieve and add lemon juice, together with a little gin, Bacardi or vodka to taste. Peel, core and quarter a couple of ripe pears and slice each quarter into thin, elegant slices. As you do so, dip each slice into a little of whichever alcohol you're using, to prevent discoloration. Flood each plate with a central stem of persimmon sauce, arrange the pear slices up the stem, Olympic torch fashion. At its base make a pedestal of three opaque lychees, tinned or fresh. Serve soon after making.

PEARS IN BLACKCURRANT SAUCE

Simmer 8 oz / 225 g blackcurrants in 10 fl oz / 300 ml water until soft, 5 minutes should be ample. Purée until smooth and then sieve to remove the debris, making sure to push through as much of the thick juice as possible. Sweeten to taste with 2–3 tablespoons of soft brown sugar. Peel, core and halve 2 large or 4 medium ripe but firm pears and arrange in a pan in a single layer. Cover with the purée and poach gently, lid slightly ajar, until the pears are soft, basting occasionally with the sauce. How long depends on your pears, anything from 15–25 minutes. The sauce meanwhile will reduce to a thick purée and acquire a glossy sheen. If the pears take longer than anticipated, keep your eye on the sauce, adding a little more water if necessary. Allow to cool and serve cold, in plain white dishes if you can, spooning the sauce over and around the pears.

SUMMER PUDDING

One of our best desserts, packed full of fibre and vitamins. A recipe seems almost superfluous; we make it instinctively, as we boil an egg or make tea. The choice of fruit is yours. Over the years I have settled on raspberries and no more than a quarter of blackcurrants and redcurrants, but I should hate to get into an argument about it. But do use good bread.

generous 1½–2 lb / 675–900 g ripe soft fruits, predominantly raspberries with redcurrants, blackcurrants and strawberries to taste; 1–2 oz / 30–60 g soft brown sugar; light wheatmeal or strong, unbleached white loaf; *crème de cassis* or raspberry liqueur (optional).

Line a 1 pint / 600 ml capacity pudding basin with slices of 1–2 day old bread, crusts removed, and making sure there are no gaps whatsoever. My preference is for thinly sliced bread but most other recipes call for the usual sandwich thickness. Rest assured, the pudding does not collapse if its walls are a little thinner. Cook the fruit, with sugar to taste, very briefly – 2 or 3 minutes – just enough for some of the juices to run. Spoon most of the fruit and some of its juice into the basin, stopping short of the brim, as otherwise too much will ooze out when the pudding is weighted. Cover completely with more bread, again being scrupulous about filling in any gaps, put a saucer underneath to catch any drips and another the same size as the pudding on top. Place a 3 lb / 1½ kg weight on top of that and leave in the refrigerator for at least 24 hours, longer if it suits. Purée the remaining fruit, sieve and add a measure of *crème de cassis* or raspberry liqueur. Cover with cling film and leave in the refrigerator until required.

When the time comes to serve the pudding, loosen it first with a spatula, slipping it round the sides of the basin. Place an inverted plate on top, turn the whole thing upside down and give it a shake. The pudding should come out cleanly. Spoon a little of the sauce over the top, decorate with a few fresh berries, and serve the rest of the sauce separately. Cream is the usual accompaniment for summer pudding. I prefer it plain.

HOME-MADE JELLIES

Home-made jellies, wobbly rather than rubbery and made with real ingredients, are a delight and a treat, however old or young you are. The formula is simple and always the same. Take any freshly squeezed citrus juice or clear soft fruit juice (made by simmering the fruit gently and briefly) or any sieved fresh fruit purée. Sweeten to taste, add dissolved gelatine and pour into wet moulds to set. Additional flavourings can be added to suit.

The only problem may be the gelatine. Its faintly gluey after-taste can easily mask the delicious freshness of the fruit. My inclination is to abandon tradition and not bother with a set strong enough to turn out but, instead, to pour the jelly into individual stemmed glasses. It's a good idea also to add a splash of the appropriate alcohol. It helps disguise the flavour of the gelatine.

Most liquids set with gelatine in about 4 hours in the refrigerator. The full setting-power is reached after about 12 hours, a point worth bearing in mind, particularly for these lightly-set jellies. In warm weather keep them well-chilled. As a rule of thumb, one packet of gelatine, weighing approximately ½ oz / 15 g – it may say less on the packet but when weighed seems always to be this amount – and which contains 4 teaspoons, will set 1 pint / 600 ml of liquid to a firm jelly. Increasing the liquid content by 3–4 fl oz / 90–120 ml gives a slightly softer set, which I prefer.

RASPBERRY CLOUD

An untraditional, cloudy jelly which easily adapts to any fruit which has bulk and purées successfully [4–6 servings].

12 oz / 340 g raspberries; approx 15 fl oz / 450 ml mineral water; 2–3 oz / 60–90 g sugar; ½ oz packet / scant 15 g / 4 teaspoons powdered

gelatine; 2–3 tablespoons raspberry liqueur, *crème de cassis*, or other appropriate spirit; 6 tablespoons hot water.

Purée the raspberries with ½ pint / 300 ml of the mineral water, sieve, pressing through everything except the pips, and make up to a generous 1 pint / 600 ml with more of the water. Add the liqueur and sugar to taste and stir until dissolved. Sprinkle the gelatine into a jug containing the hot water and set in a pan of hot water over a low heat. Stir until the gelatine is completely dissolved, pour on some of the raspberry juice, stirring constantly, and then tip the mixture back into the rest of the raspberry juice. Mix thoroughly, check for final taste and sweetness and pour into individual dishes to set. The mixture will separate slightly, leaving a clear layer on the bottom with a foamy cloud on top. Leave plain or decorate with a few fresh raspberries, and serve well-chilled. For a more intense flavour, increase the quantity of the raspberries to 1 lb / 450 g and alter the quantity of water accordingly.

MELISSA JELLY

A sophisticated, night-time jelly to serve as an end to a grander than usual evening meal [4–6 servings].

1½–2 oz / 45–60 g lemon balm, thoroughly washed and dried, or sweet vermouth (see method); 12 fl oz / 360 ml medium sweet wine, German for preference; 2–2½ oz / 60–75 g caster sugar; 6 fl oz / 180 ml mineral water; 2 tablespoons strained lemon juice; 6 tablespoons hot water; ½ oz packet / 15 g / 4 teaspoons powdered gelatine.

Macerate the lemon balm in the wine for 45 minutes or until the wine becomes sufficiently perfumed with the scent of melissa. Aim for a pronounced but not too aggressive tang. Strain, pressing through the juices, and stir in the lemon juice. If no lemon balm is available, substitute about 2 fl oz / 60 ml of the wine with a good vermouth. Add the mineral water and sugar to taste, stirring until completely dissolved. Mix the gelatine with the hot water in a jug as in the previous recipe, pour in the wine mixture and stir thoroughly. Taste and make any alterations to sweetness and pour into elegant, stemmed glasses to set. Decorate with a tiny sprig of lemon balm or scented geranium leaf just before serving.

Alternatively – this stretches the jelly further – pour the jelly into a shallow bowl to set, chop it roughly and serve spooned over peeled and de-seeded grapes piled neatly into individual glasses. Or arrange the roughly chopped jelly in a serving dish, dot with grapes and decorate with a fringe of scented geranium leaves.

YOGHURT CUSTARD

Yoghurt makes excellent custard, slightly sharp and less cloying than the usual kind. Neither does it curdle, a blessing when proper custard is called for but there's precious little time to attend to its cooking.

For each person allow 1 large egg yolk, 3–4 fl oz / 90–120 ml plain home-made yoghurt and a generous teaspoon or slightly more of honey. Put all the ingredients into a small pan over a gentle heat and keep stirring until the mixture comes to the boil and has thickened. Serve on its own or with fruit and other puddings. It's excellent cold, light and creamy when set. For a grander sweet, perfume it with elderflowers, geranium leaves or rose water, and serve in little custard cups or ramekin dishes.

TEA CREAM

A dessert for those who like a mild and gentle finish to their meal. This version is based on the one which appeared in Jane Grigson's *British Cookery* which she, in turn, adapted from that given by John Farley in 1783. It is, in effect, no more than up-market junket and is wholly delicious. Green or gunpowder tea is available from Chinese supermarkets. It has a fine flavour, exactly right after a meal for those who don't want coffee.

15 fl oz / 450 ml milk; 5 fl oz / 150 ml single cream; $\frac{1}{4}$ oz / $7\frac{1}{2}$ g (approx. 4 teaspoons) gunpowder tea; 1–2 teaspoons sugar; 1 junket tablet crushed and dissolved in 1 tablespoon warm water.

Bring the milk to the boil and stir in the tea – its bullet-like leaves unfurl dramatically. Remove from the heat and let the tea infuse for 2–3 minutes until the flavour seems right remembering that the cream will soften the final taste slightly. Pour the milk through a sieve into a pan, pressing the leaves lightly to extract the greenish drops of liquid, and stir in the cream. Sweeten very slightly – a teaspoon or so changes the flavour quite markedly and can be left out if you prefer – and then check the temperature. It needs to be at blood heat, 38°C (98°F), so cool or reheat as necessary. Add the dissolved junket tablet, stir for a few seconds and pour into suitably elegant serving dishes or glasses which will show off the faint green-grey of the cream to its best advantage. Leave to set in a cool place or the refrigerator. Decorate discreetly just before serving. Mrs Grigson suggests a pinch of strained tea leaves in the centre, but adds that one could do better. [Serves 6.]

EVERLASTING SYLLABUB

Two cream-based desserts worth making are gooseberry fool and syllabub. I'd be hard put to choose between the two, but syllabub would probably win. As its name implies, it keeps well, even improving with age. Recipes vary but only in detail. Most, like mine, are based on the one Elizabeth David gives in her booklet *Syllabubs and Fruit Fools,* first published in 1969. I will never understand why something so simple and easy is made so badly in restaurants. All it wants is wine, lemon juice, sugar and cream. What is difficult about that?

4 fl oz / scant 120 ml medium sweet wine; 2 tablespoons brandy; rind of 1 well-scrubbed lemon; 1 tablespoon strained lemon juice; 1–1½ oz / 30–45 g sugar; 5 fl oz / 150 ml double cream.

Macerate the first four ingredients overnight. Next day, strain the mixture into a large bowl and stir in sugar to taste. Keep stirring until the sugar has completely dissolved. Pour the cream on to the mixture in a steady stream, stirring gently as you go. Now, using a balloon whisk, begin whisking firmly but lightly and unhurriedly. The mixture doubles in size and turns into a billowy cloud of creamy foam. Be careful not to overwhip, for the cream will turn grainy and your syllabub be ruined. Spoon into dainty glasses and leave in a cool place until required. It will keep for a week or so. Cover with cling film and store in the refrigerator. Decorations aren't really necessary, though a couple of wisp-like lemon curls never go amiss.

You will note that the proportion of liquid to cream is higher here than in other modern recipes. Whilst this makes for added lightness and volume, it also makes it more fragile. This syllabub has a tendency to separate, leaving a little alcoholic pool of liquid in the bottom of the glass or bowl, reminiscent, I imagine, of the early style syllabubs, which were more of a drink than a solid confection. I find this a bonus but others may find it a fault. If so, keep the syllabub in the bowl and re-whip very cautiously just before serving. [Serves 4–6].

STRAWBERRY SOUFFLÉ

An excellent foolproof soufflé, from Stafford Whiteaker's *The Compleat Strawberry*, published in 1985. I have reduced the sugar content and altered the proportions slightly. The recipe adapts well to other soft fruits.

Purée a generous 8 oz / 225 g of very ripe strawberries in a blender. Cook gently with 1 oz / 30 g sugar for a few minutes until the mixture starts to thicken. Allow to cool and then gently fold in two stiffly beaten egg whites. Pile into 4 individual soufflé dishes, mounding the mixture well over the top. Alternatively use a larger dish, but make sure it is full. Carefully place in a preheated oven, 170–180°C / 330–350°F / gas mark 4, and cook for about 7–10 minutes until well risen and lightly brown on top. Have 4 small plates ready to stand the soufflés on, and serve immediately.

SWEET LIQUEUR SOUFFLÉS

A couple of years ago, the BBC ran a 'World of Cooking' series. From Chartreuse in France came this soufflé – a frothy extravaganza of alcoholic foam. I have since made it many times when the oven is hot and egg whites are going spare. This is my version.

2 egg yolks; 4 egg whites; 2 tablespoons caster sugar; 3–4 tablespoons liqueur, e.g. Grand Marnier or Chartreuse.

Butter a large flat serving dish which will stand a hot oven and show off the soufflé nicely. Using an electric whisk, cream the egg yolks with half the sugar until pale, thick and mousse-like. Add the liqueur and briefly beat again. Whisk the egg whites to a soft snow, tip in the rest of the sugar and continue whisking until very stiff and shiny. Lightly fold the two mixtures together. Don't worry about lumps of egg white, the idea is to disturb the mixture as little as possible. Pile on to the serving dish – aim for a billowy effect – sprinkle sparingly with extra sugar and cook in the centre of a preheated hot oven, 200°C / 400°F / gas mark 6, for 9–10 minutes. The soufflé is done when well risen and the surface slightly browned. Don't be tempted to overcook to dryness. It should be moist and no more than comfortably warm. Serve immediately and have hot plates at the ready.

Half quantities, with slightly shorter cooking times, make a light, quickly-made dessert for two. For a delicious change, sprinkle the base with a few slices of fresh fruits, strawberries, cherries, pears or peaches, or use some of the fruit from a home-made liqueur. [Serves 3–4.]

COCONUT SORBET

For those who are fond of coconut, an idea from *Great Desserts*, published in 1983. The sorbet is a brilliant snow-white, rich and creamy in texture. Think of it as a cream ice and serve in small portions with sliced fresh fruit – mangoes, peaches – or a fresh fruit sauce such as raspberry or banana.

8 fl oz / 240 ml tinned coconut milk; 5 fl oz / 150 ml mineral water; 2 tablespoons rum or Bacardi; 2 egg whites; 2 oz / 60 g caster sugar.

Mix the coconut milk – should it have separated in the tin, blend it first to a smooth cream – with the mineral water and rum or Bacardi. Whip the egg whites to a soft snow, add the sugar and whisk again until thick and shiny. Gently but thoroughly fold the egg whites into the coconut mixture and freeze until the sides have set but the centre is still liquid. Beat again till smooth and freeze until required. Allow to soften slightly before serving.

LEMON AND BLACKCURRANT WATER ICE

Blackcurrant leaves, especially in their first flush of youth in late spring, are impregnated with a delicate and unmistakable fragrance of the fruit to come. They're one of many leaves that have culinary possibilities and they make a most refreshing water ice – sharp, tangy and full of the scent of summer.

20 fl oz / 600 ml water; 8 oz / 225 g sugar; rind of 2 lemons, well-scrubbed, plus the strained juice; good handful of washed blackcurrant leaves; stiffly beaten egg white.

Gently simmer the lemon rind, water and sugar for 5–7 minutes. Take off the heat, add the blackcurrant leaves, shaken free of any moisture, and leave to infuse until the syrup has cooled. Strain, pressing the leaves against the sieve. Add the lemon juice and freeze until almost solid but still slightly liquid in the centre. Beat until smooth, in a blender or food processor if you can, fold in the stiffly beaten egg white and freeze until firm. Scoop out portions of the water ice with a rounded spoon or an ice-cream spoon and serve on a bed of blackcurrant leaves. Or serve in glasses or with sliced fruits. Pearly currants make a pretty garnish. [Serves 6–8.]

INDEX